Yul Brynner

Yul Brynner

— THE — INSCRUTABLE — KING —

Jhan Robbins

DODD, MEAD & COMPANY
New York

Published by Dodd, Mead & Company, Inc.
71 Fifth Avenue, New York, New York 10003
Distributed in Canada by
McClelland and Stewart Limited, Toronto
Manufactured in the United States of America
Designed by Mark Bergeron
First Edition

1 2 3 4 5 6 7 8 9 10

Library of Congress Cataloging-in-Publication Data

Robbins, Jhan.
    Yul Brynner : the inscrutable king.

    Includes index.
    1. Brynner, Yul.   2. Actors—United States—Biography.
I. Title.
PN2287.B74R6   1987   792'.028'0924 [B]   87-6679
ISBN 0-396-08675-6

Contents

To Mary Martin,
whose perceptivity enabled her to spot
a consummate star performer.

Acknowledgments

MANY people aided me in writing this biography—their names and contributions appear in the text. Most of them were candid and honest in presenting their recollections. I owe a special debt to my wife Sallie Prugh who made many invaluable suggestions, Mary Martin who brought Yul Brynner to the world's attention, Carole Silverman whose collection of Brynner memorabilia is massive, Cynthia Vartan and June Reno for their editing skill, researchers Chris Hare and Elizabeth Whisnant, Polly Brown for her typing.

Preface

MY initial meeting with the King was regally staged—by him. He was dressed as the sovereign of Siam in a red silk robe. I felt he expected me to fall to my knees. It was in the early 1950s and I had just started working for the New York *Herald Tribune*. The editor had assigned me to write a story about the actor whose clean-shaven head was rapidly becoming as celebrated as the Eisenhower grin. I had been warned that Brynner was his own best press agent; that rarely had a self-created image received greater prominence or told more elaborate, spurious tales. *The World Almanac* listed him as having been born in 1915; *Current Biography*, 1917; and *Who's Who*, 1920.

"He won't fool me!" I said. There is no one more worldy-wise than a young reporter. At the outset of the interview my antagonism was high. Quickly, however, his naked skull, mesmerizing eyes, and flaming nostrils rolled it over. When he learned that my first name—*Jhan*—contained a silent *h*, he convinced me that we were kindred souls because his name also possessed a silent *h*.

"My true name is Taidge Khan, Jr.," he said. "The blood of Ghengis Khan flows through my viens . . . My father was a leading adviser to the Czar . . . I ran away from home at age thirteen to join the circus . . . I have a Ph.D. from the Sorbonne . . . The money I earn from acting helps support my destitute gypsy family."

Obediently, I wrote down everything he said. The King had swayed me and gained another trusting admirer. I filed the story. Later that evening, I had second thoughts about my gullibility. To help submerge my annoyance I visited Bleeck's, a bar that was frequented by newspapermen and theatrical people. Like Brynner it had given itself a prestigious name, "The Artists and Writers Club."

Richard Maney, a well-known Broadway press agent, was sitting on the stool next to me. When I told him how I had been duped by Brynner, he patted my shoulder. "Welcome aboard," he said kindly. "I'll wager that half the people in this saloon have had similar experiences." Then he grimaced as he added, "That includes me. Once when I was working on a show he was in, I asked him about his origin. In three minutes flat he tossed out three different versions. What's more, I found myself believing all three. Yul never tells a simple lie. Perhaps fascinating fabrications? Many, however, have some truth to them. The challenge is to discover which ones are real."

Over the years I saw Brynner often. I learned that in addition to his being closely identified with the role of king, he excelled in many other areas:

- He had been one of the early television directors and was responsible for some of the top shows.
- The United Nations considered him a prized special ambassador.
- He was an expert photographer—pictures he had taken appeared regularly in national magazines.
- Furniture designed and built by him had been displayed by the Museum of Modern Art.

- He lectured frequently at philatelic conventions. His stamp collection was appraised at a quarter of a million dollars.
- Yul's name had been romantically linked with dozens of the most glamorous, international actresses.
- He married four lovely looking and extremely talented women.
- The Escofier Society of France had called him a distinguished gourmet.
- He was a champion water skier—had jumped eighty-five feet.
- Argentina named an alcoholic drink after him.

In succeeding interviews I had with Brynner, he told me dozens of intriguing but conflicting stories. Some of them did not appear in chronological order. He boasted that he didn't live that way. "Show me a person who thinks systematically," he said, "and I'll show you a dull, bloody bore."

At times the man and the myth became so inseparable they were difficult to unhook. But everything about him is undeniably colorful and romantic and well worth recalling. So let's enjoy.

Jhan Robbins
Columbia, S.C.

CHAPTER ONE

Just a Clean-Cut Mongolian Boy

AT the age of sixty-five going on seventy, Yul Brynner presented himself as an exotic Oriental. If you had any doubts, you only had to ask him. I did. "I'm a typical Mongolian boy," he replied. "Gifted, golden-voiced, creative, discreet, attractive to women. Although, at the present time, somewhat ill."

He went on to say, tossing his head arrogantly, that a cheerful aspect of being sick is that there is nothing like it for taking weight off the middle. He tightened the sash on his black cashmere smoking jacket. It was embroidered in gold thread with plunging dragons.

In September 1983 doctors had told him that his customary five packs of cigarettes a day had brought on inoperable cancer. They said bluntly that he should put his affairs in order, that he likely had about two months to live. He confounded them by spending the next two years singing and dancing in the role in which he had made his major mark, and by plainly enjoying his young wife.

"I'll die in bed or on the stage," he said. "Where else is there to be?"

Shortly before his death in 1985, the veteran stage and screen actor closed a triumphant revival of *The King and I*.

He had first appeared in the show thirty-four years before; 4,625 performances later, he waved imperiously as the final curtain came down and the sentimental audience sang *Auld Lang Syne*. As he walked to his dressing room he was handed a telegram from Ronald Reagan. "I've never had anything run that long," the President's message said. "My job keeps me booked for only eight years. But I know something of the bittersweet feeling one can have when a project is wrapped . . . Yours has been a mysterious and fascinating life."

Brynner had always done his best to add to the intriguing image he had created. He gave various accounts of his origin, birthplace, background, and childhood. Bemused reporters, shrewd columnists, and roaring city editors heard in turn that he was Mongolian, Russian, Romany gypsy, and Siberian. With Chinese connections. When caught with an obvious contradiction, he'd look amused and say, "I'm a joint, worldwide, national, and international citizen of the earth."

He spoke accented, idiomatic English that playwright Noël Coward once described as "rhythmical Americanese marinated in borscht." Yul was also fluent in Russian, French, Chinese, Mongolian, Romany gypsy, and Korean. His conversation was sprinkled with words and phrases of Yiddish, German, Greek, Italian, and Japanese. He sang melancholy bars of what he said were Siberian gypsy folk songs.

"Gypsies were Indo-Europeans," protested theatrical reporter Burton Rascoe. "They never got as far north as Siberia."

"That's what you think!" Yul said and went on singing.

He may have succeeded in making it difficult to determine his real birthday and birthplace. However, the entry on a 1939 passport application said that he was born in Vladivostok in Czarist Russia on July 7, 1915. In 1976, while rehearsing for *The King and I* revival, he had his press agent distribute photocopies of a page from his Swiss passport. It listed his birthday as July 11, 1920. When confronted with the discrepancy, he said, "Ordinary mortals need but one birthday."

His mother was part Russian; his father part Swiss. At the time, the actor with the famous shaved head spelled his name Youl Bryner.

It was altered years later by a New York theatrical agent who told him that Youl sounded too much like "you-all," and Bryner as though he was soaked in brine and pickled. He became Yul Brynner, pronounced *Yool Brinner*.

The Swiss relationship was through his paternal grandfather, August Bryner, a native of Geneva, a counsel who worked in Czarist Russia for the diplomatic corps. The family was upper-middle class. August's job was to look after the Swiss interests in coal and the newly burgeoning oil wells in the shorelands at the north end of the Sea of Japan.

Yul's grandfather was stationed on the sizable island of Sakhalin, which was Russian in the north and Japanese in the south. August was married to Nadia Verasonova, a Romanian gypsy. This validates Brynner's claim to being part gypsy.

August and Nadia had trouble with their youngest son, Boris, who was to become Yul's father. Boris, beginning at about age seventeen, lived the sporting life. Sakhalin was filled with moneyed aristocrats who absented themselves from the joint alarms of political unrest in Moscow and St. Petersburg and the military bristles of the German kaiser a little farther to the west. With an imperious attitude of "eat, drink, and be merry" and the French theory about life in general, a section of the island glittered like today's Monaco. It encompassed jeweled women, titled gentry, the delicate fragrance of good wine, and the rattle of gaming boards. This was in sharp contrast to the penal colonies that had been established on the island. The Bryners employed several ex-convicts as house servants.

Boris became involved, so Yul related, in a double love affair with twin countesses twelve years older than he. They lived in twin manor houses that were several hundred feet apart. Boris crossed to and fro.

Each sister was led to believe that she was the favorite. But he publicly rejected both of them by escorting another woman, the pretty daughter of one of the convicts, to a local party. Four days later, in the early morning, the twin countesses climbed aboard a trunkline of the Orient Express and flung themselves from opposite ends of the observation platform of the moving train. It was traveling slowly, about ten miles per hour. They survived, with a few broken ribs and contusions. None were on the face, as they had prudently wrapped their heads in towels. Each had posted an angry, passionate letter to Boris and the local newspaper.

Shortly after the scandal broke, Yul's father was packed off to a university in Odessa to study engineering. It was in the middle of the term and housing was difficult to come by. One of the professors pitied the young man and invited him to board in his house. A grateful Boris promptly impregnated the teacher's wife. Again he was forced to flee. This time, his humiliated parents sent him to a school in St. Petersburg.

There at a masquerade ball he met Maria Blagovidova, a pretty Greek-Russian drama student at the St. Petersburg Conservatory. He had come dressed as Julius Caesar; she as Cleopatra. "Naturally," said Yul, "they were slated to become lovers."

Maria and Boris were married ten weeks later. She was nineteen, he twenty-three. At the time of the wedding, friends described the union in the downstairs vulgarity of the day: "Joined in holy wedlock by the breaking of a thin-skinned bag."

Yul's mother talked of returning to school after her son's birth, but the arrival of a daughter, Vera, in 1916, changed her plans. The young couple and their children lived rent-free in August's house in Sakhalin. He continued to give Boris a liberal allowance. Maria showed her displeasure over the arrangement by moving out of her husband's bedroom. Boris retaliated by becoming involved with several local women. When Yul was five years old, his parents decided to separate.

Boris remained in Sakhalin, where his father had given him money to start an export-import business. The Russian Revolution took some time to drift east. Switzerland, neutral and channeling funds to aristocrats, Mensheviks and Bolsheviks alike, kept consul August in place.

Maria took the two small children to Manchuria. She settled in Harbin. "It had a large Russian population," Yul said. "Even Russian-speaking policemen." The young Yul had a habit of slipping away from his mother and showing up at the police station. "I'm the Czar's grandson," he'd say. "I live in a palace." His mother grew accustomed to seeing Yul arrive at the door, his ear pinched between a policeman's thumb and finger. "Here's the Czarevitch—again," the policeman would say resignedly.

Brynner rarely discussed his early years unless he had consumed large amounts of Scotch or vodka. Then he'd become very voluble. "When we had just arrived in Harbin, I had a friend named Gregory," Yul recalled. "Although he was a few years older, we played together. But then he became sick. I was told that it was a bad cold and he would soon get well. A few days later he died. That was the first real grief I suffered. People who claim that kids quickly get over sorrow are bloody fools. They don't know what they're talking about. To this day I often think of Gregory."

Shortly after his young friend died, an incident occurred that may have played a significant role in Brynner's life. Yul's mother had given her son a very hot bowl of porridge for breakfast. "I had just finished it when I started coughing," he said. "No matter how hard I tried I couldn't stop. My mother yelled that I had eaten it too fast and as a result it had gone down the wrong pipe."

Maria became alarmed when two hours later he was still coughing. "She took me to the hospital," Yul said. "I was there for nearly a week, but they never found out what was wrong with me. No thanks to them, I had stopped coughing that night."

The doctor wanted to discharge him, but his mother insisted that her son be kept for observation. "In all that time," Yul said, "they didn't learn a solitary thing. But I made a discovery—the minute I stopped coughing, I was no longer considered a special attraction. So I pretended the coughing spell had returned. *Plop!* I was a celebrity again. The next day I tried a new ruse. I told the doctor that I had suddenly gone blind—I couldn't see a solitary thing. He tried all kinds of tricks to trip me up. But I kept on with my blind act so effectively that he actually gave me a white cane. He took it away the next day when I said my sight had miraculously returned."

Yul's sister Vera, who became a distinguished opera singer, said, "My mother believed that he thrived on mystery and defiance from the moment he was born." Vera adored her brother, and friends say that he felt the same way about her. However, she admitted that she was often baffled by him. Sometimes he referred to her as his half sister or stepsister. "The truth is that we had the same mother and father," she said. "But if he wants to create fantasies about us, I suppose it's his right."

He discouraged Vera from discussing his background. All she would reveal were anecdotes from his school days. "Yul would go to class wearing different-colored stockings —one blue and one red," she said, "or two different-colored shoes. Anything to attract attention. Once, my mother bought him a one-piece, black bathing suit. At the time it was customary to wear a suit that covered your entire body. Yul didn't think that was the right style for him. So he got a pair of shears and cut it way down. My brother should be credited for fashioning the first pair of men's bathing briefs."

A teacher asked seven-year-old Yul to draw a picture of a tranquil outdoor scene. He did. "But only Charles Addams or Salvador Dali would have approved," Vera said. "He drew a giant ant eating the roof of a black-draped castle that resembled the Czar's palace. When he was scolded, he asked innocently, 'Doesn't everybody have to eat? Even ants?' He said it in such a way that my mother was sent for."

That Christmas, Brynner was given a guitar. "He kept practicing all the time," Vera recalled. "Also kept bragging how good he was. Finally, he was invited to appear in a school recital. Parents attended. When his turn came he walked slowly to the center of the stage, scorning a chair that had been put there for him. Instead, he sat on the floor and began to sing and strum the guitar. The words were pure gibberish. He announced they were old-fashioned gypsy melodies. Everybody believed him. People usually do. Yul was the King long before he became king of Siam."

In the early thirties, Maria Bryner and the two children moved to Paris. They had very little money and kept shifting from one tiny apartment to another, leaving a puddle of unpaid neighborhood debts behind. Boris had promised to send monthly checks, but after a year they ceased coming. Maria got a job as a saleswoman in a dress shop. She received eight dollars a week. The owner, a sixty-one-year-old widower, wanted to marry her. She felt that he was too old to make a suitable father. When she rejected the proposal she was fired. Her next job was in a hat shop. An employee closer to her age started dating her. The romance ended when Yul showed his displeasure by locking the suitor in a closet.

Despite his family's poverty, Brynner felt that the time he lived in Paris was the most meaningful period in his life. "I shall always be grateful to France for teaching me the Gallic way of living," he said. "That experience has made me a Francophile forever, even if the pendulum used to swing from happy to sad—rarely in between. Nothing in France is in between."

Yul claimed that he had won an athletic scholarship to a private boarding school. "They were delighted when I became a student," he said. "I was their star athlete in soccer, swimming, and track. But the truth is that I never enjoyed sports, except water-skiing." There aren't any records that indicate his enrollment, but among his possessions is a silver medal for track excellence. Unfortunately, the name of the donor is illegible.

"I became bored with school when I was thirteen," Yul said. "That's when I ran away to join the circus."

"Not so," said Paul Mueller, whose family operated the food concession of Paris's famous *Cirque d'Hiver*. "When I met Yul he was exactly the same age I was, and I was going on eighteen. The reason I'm so sure is that when he discovered our birthdays were only three days apart, we celebrated them together. My mother used to say we were practically twins."

Thirteen—or eighteen—Yul, who greatly resembled his father, was equally precocious. Older women also singled him out. "He started as a clown trainee," Mueller said. "But then he met Eva, who was at least ten years his senior. She and her husband, Otto, did a spectacular high-wire act. She was crazy about Yul. He'd tell me in great detail everything that happened between them—and believe me, it was a lot. He pestered her to make him a flyer."

Mueller remembered the first time Brynner performed in public. "Yul behaved as if had been operating in air all of his life," he said. "When he came down he told me, 'Paul, I suppose I can do anything I want to try.' I suppose he could."

July and August of each year meant the closing of the

circus. "Air-conditioning was brand new and pretty expensive," Brynner said. "So naturally it wasn't installed. When it got too hot to attract customers we'd be given a vacation —without pay. That taught me a valuable lesson about employers—all of them are cheapskates."

Yul's first fill-in job was singing in a Left Bank nightclub. "We didn't get paid," Yul recalled. "If the customers liked the way we performed they'd toss coins at us. Some nights the pickings were so small that I decided to look elsewhere."

He became a substitute player with a jai alai team. His career ended when the team had to disband because of poor attendance. I wasn't very unhappy when it did," Brynner said. "I never did like the game. I took the job because of the owner's daughter. She made her father hire me."

He finished the season as a lifeguard on the beach at Biarritz. "I liked this job much better," Yul said. "Every Sunday night the married men would return to the city. Their blasé wives made it very clear they wanted companionship. They were particularly attracted to the lifeguards. So we obliged."

One of the women, a mother of two teenagers, bought Yul shirts and ties. He would tell her that she didn't have to purchase his attention. However, he kept right on accepting the gifts. He got so many presents that he began selling them to the other lifeguards. Yul felt that the woman's husband was probably wise to what was going on, but pretended to be unaware. "I think he had a mistress that he was keeping and was happy not to be questioned about her."

Every September Brynner returned to the circus, where he remained for three years. Eva was replaced by her cousin Bella, another trapeze performer. "Then it happened," Yul said. "A rope accidentally broke and I fell sideways out of the net against some parallel bars."

Mueller disagreed. "His rope didn't break accidentally," he said. "It was deliberately cut by a jealous woman!"

Whatever caused it, Brynner suffered several dozen fractures, and wore a plaster cast for months. He was told he'd be crippled for life. "I was devastated," he said. "Nothing since has ever approached the joys of flying on trapeze bars. It was an exhilarating feeling. When I was doing it I felt so free. But I knew that I had to find some less-strenuous line of work. At the time the Moscow Art Theater, under the supervision of Michael Chekhov, was touring France."

Yul decided to take a look. "What I saw changed my life forever," he said. "Chekhov had developed Stanislavsky's ideas into something far more effective. The result was the most extraordinary acting I've ever seen."

Brynner was so intrigued that he went backstage. "Chekhov talked to me for a long time," Yul said. "He was undoubtedly the most talented man I've ever known. I returned the next night and the next and the next. I saw much of his repertory: *Inspector General, Eric the Fourteenth, Hamlet.* But soon he left France to start an acting school in England. I wanted to follow but lack of funds stopped me. It was the only time that I've allowed money to keep me from doing something I really wanted. I've never let it happen again."

Instead, Brynner became an unpaid apprentice with the Paris repertory company of Georges and Ludmilla Pitoeff, the Lunt and Fontanne of France. "While I closely observed their every move, I was given loads of menial jobs—sweeping floors, dusting props, going out for coffee."

Eventually, Brynner was promoted to moving scenery and helping fashion wigs. He received his first review because of a hairpiece. Yul had assisted in making a Madame Pompadour wig for one of the stars. A critic raved about it. He wrote that the wig was far better than the performance given by the actress who wore it.

Yul was finally given some minor roles. His biggest assignment—and the one he said he hated the most—was playing a paramour in *Camille.* "I detested that part," he said. "Young lovers are the most hateful bunch of snobs in literature and the theater."

His displeasure must have showed. "Madame Pitoeff told me that I was awful," he said. "I've always felt that lover roles are the least interesting thing to play. It's far, far better to be a lover off the stage than on it. You need time to get inside a woman's skin to really understand her."

He recognized the Freudian slip, but offered no apology; he just smiled and fashioned a tent out of his fingertips. He used the episode to launch into his theory about attracting women. "Long ago," he said, "I discovered that evoking pity but at the same time being disdainful works with most ladies. In those days it wasn't difficult to make them feel sorry for me—I weighed about 120 pounds. They would offer to take me home. Before I'd agree, I'd make them promise to give me a large breakfast in the morning. I can't recall a single refusal. They were more than satisfied by my approach. It seemed to excite them."

Once, however, it worked too well. "I met this red-haired, rich divorcée in a Montmartre nightclub," he said. "After a night of lovemaking, she had her maid serve me breakfast in bed—champagne and eggs. I threw up."

Brynner saw the woman several more times. The affair ended when two detectives arrived at the repertory theater to question him. The woman had been strangled, and he was the chief suspect. "Luckily, I had proof I'd been out of town when the murder occurred," Yul said. "Still, I was worried."

Jean Levin, who later became an award-winning film director, was a fellow apprentice in the Pitoeff company. "That incident really shook him," he said. "For days he went around looking like a walking ghost. He told me that he'd never glance at another woman again—that he had learned his lesson. But right after they caught the real killer, Yul asked me if I'd join him on a double date. He was mercurial about most things. Especially where women were concerned."

Several male members of the company joined the loyalists who were fighting in the Spanish Civil War. Among them was Levin. "Yul wanted to enlist, but a severe case of influenza kept him from going. A few weeks later when he recovered, he changed his mind—the Pitoeffs had selected him for a major role in one of the plays."

Levin believes that Yul was sorry that his ailment had been something as ordinary as influenza. "He desperately wanted a more dramatic illness," he said. "There was a girl in our troupe who was dying from TB. I'm sure the main reason he dated her was that he wanted to be reported as loving so much as to risk it. He used to tell me that unless you did something conspicuous you'd be lost in the crowd."

Levin fought in Spain for two months. The fingers on his left hand were amputated. "At first I was uneasy about them," he said. " 'Don't be!' Yul would shout. 'Call attention to it!' He bought me a set of Greek worry beads to advertise my missing fingers. Everything he did had to be dramatic. I remember the first time I became aware of him. It was when a delivery man made an anti-Semitic remark about me. I have a large, hooked nose that people associate with Jews. I pretended not to hear the insult. Not Yul! He knocked the man down and refused to let him up until he kissed my shoes."

When the Nazis invaded Poland, Yul tried to join the French army. He was rejected because of his circus injuries. "But that didn't end it," Levin said. "I wasn't too surprised when he told me that he planned on kidnapping the chief of staff and make him listen to reason. He forgot about his scheme when he received an invitation from his father to visit him in Peking."

Yul's father had settled in China after fleeing the Russian Revolution. His business had prospered, but was now the property of the new Soviet government. He had started a smaller import-export operation in Peking. "I accepted the invitation," Yul said. "For both of us it was meaningful. We hadn't really known each other before. I hardly recognized him. He had aged a great deal and now had a pot belly. But now that I was older I could appreciate some of his qualities. He was a charming conversationalist. Arrogant, but underneath he was really quite gentle. What's more, I realized that he really liked me. There is a certain liberation that comes with maturity—you can see and understand so much more."

Yul told beguiling stories that supposedly happened during that visit. "My father had befriended a young Chinese law professor who had strong political differences with the ruling authorities," he said. "So much so that he was given a lengthy jail sentence. Somehow he had managed to escape and made his way to my father's house. We hid him in the attic until my father could build a large wooden chest. I helped. We drilled tiny holes in each corner, then the man stepped in and lay down flat. Since my father shipped out large crates in the course of his business, he wasn't questioned. The chest was posted to Switzerland, where my father had a branch. When the man arrived there safely, his thankful family insisted on giving us presents."

At this point in the story, Yul looked knowingly at a large jade bust of Buddha he had in his dressing room. The tip of the statue's nose was chipped off. He nodded cannily and it was assumed this was the reward he had received. Maybe so, but the records of an auction gallery that Brynner frequented listed a sale to him of a large, jade bust of Buddha that had a broken nose.

He would tell his listeners about another implausible incident that occurred in Peking. "It happened when my father and I decided to have a picnic on the outskirts of town," Yul said. "At the time it was not uncommon for destitute parents to leave their dead children on the side of the road because they were too poor to afford proper burials. So we weren't surprised when we saw a body wrapped in newspaper. But this one was different—it moved. Yes, the infant was still alive. We took it to an orphanage that was run by American missionaries. The child survived and eventually was brought to the United States."

When asked how he knew all this, he responded, "Years later, the almost-dead child, now a beautiful grown woman, auditioned for a role in *The King and I.*"

"Yul always had the ability of making the unbelievable believable," said Levin. "With him nothing was impossible."

CHAPTER TWO

The King
Comes
to America

"THERE was a story for immigrants about the streets of America being paved with gold," said Brynner. "I wasn't naive enough to fall for it. But the very first thing I found when I arrived here in 1940 was a slightly used gold filling. Apparently, someone had knocked out someone and the filling was in the gutter on Forty-second Street. It was a good omen. I sold it for five dollars."

Several months before, Yul, then in his twenties, learned that Michael Chekhov had opened an acting school in Ridgefield, Connecticut. "This time I let nothing stand in my way," Brynner said. "Call it a fancy way of scrounging, but it paid off. I wheedled and begged from everybody in sight."

He told some friends that he needed the money for his starving father in China. To others he said that his grandmother, who now lived in Connecticut, was dying. The Pitoeffs gave a benefit performance to enable him to satisfy her final wish: *"Hold my grandson one more time."*

"I still blush at some of the reasons I gave," Brynner said. "But they did result in a ticket to America."

As soon as the ship docked, he asked a customs guard to help him telephone New England. Yul told the drama teacher, "I've come to the United States to study with you, but I have no money." Chekhov remembered the dynamic young man and told him to take the next train.

Betty Mason, one of Chekhov's students, recalled how curious she was about Brynner. "The professor said that Yul was very Oriental looking. I had visions of Fu-Manchu. But he certainly wasn't anything like that. You could tell right off that he was aware of his superiority. I had never met anyone like him before. Despite his being young he had already done so much. The stories he told about his experiences sounded fabulous. He seemed to know everybody. Unlike the rest of us, he was so self-assured and knew exactly where he was going. He'd pretend to be gruff, but underneath he was a real sweetie."

Actress Beatrice Straight was Chekhov's associate. She, too, was captivated by Brynner's overwhelming confidence. "There seemed to be no adjustment he had to make to his new environment except the way he spoke English. He was the best thing that ever happened to the school."

Life with Chekhov was frenzied. Students were required to work from early morning to late night. The day sessions were devoted to popular psychology, occultism, hypnosis voice control, facial expressions, choral singing, fencing, calisthenics, and atmosphere. Evenings were spent in rehearsal. "To be an actor," Chekhov lectured, "you must be prepared to work until you can't stand it any longer."

"I thought I was used to being busy," Brynner said. "But never, never have I worked so hard. When I finally turned in, it was well past midnight. I was so tired that the pallet I slept on had but a single occupant—me!"

Yul's room would have delighted the most established Bedouin. Ornate rugs hung on the walls, striped red and orange drapes covered the ceiling, garishly colored pillows were tossed around casually, and two massive ceramic urns guarded the entrance. "Each time I went into that room," said Betty Mason, "I felt as if I were in an Arab harem. We used to say that any female that was courageous enough to get within ten feet of his room had to be very brave. Oh, so soothingly would he persuade ladies to enter. Once, a well-known Broadway actress visited the school. When she finished giving us an inside picture of the stage, Yul was delegated to show her around. Of course, they wound up in his room. She didn't come out until an hour later. I'll always remember her breathless comment when she finally emerged: 'Why, he's a method actor—a method all his own!' "

Every Wednesday and Friday, Chekhov went to New York City. That was when Yul would rush off to a nearby art class where he'd pose for five dollars a session. "I was completely naked," he said. "But I can't see anything morally wrong with that. Because of my build, which had been developed in the circus, I was considered an excellent model."

Several years ago, one of the pictures surfaced in a magazine published by Andy Warhol. It was called "frontal nudity." When it was shown to Brynner, he remarked, "I don't mind Andy displaying me stark naked, but what burns me up is that the original was auctioned off for $800 and I didn't get a penny of it!"

When Chekhov felt that his students were ready to appear in public, he arranged a tour of college campuses. Although Brynner didn't have an automobile license, he helped drive the bus in which they traveled and slept. "As I gripped the steering wheel," he said, "I recited my lines. It took my mind off the traffic, but it didn't help much. I still sounded awful."

Yul's first speaking role was Cornwall in Shakespeare's *King Lear*. A reviewer for Columbia University described his speech as a "cross between Charlie Chan and Charles Boyer." His accent didn't improve when the Chekhov Players opened in Princeton. There a school newspaper said he sounded like "a drowning White Russian seaman who kept missing the lifebuoy that was tossed to him."

In spite of the adverse criticism, Chekhov continued to have faith in Brynner. "He promised that he'd give me the part of Fabian in *Twelfth Night*," Yul said. "I resolved that I wouldn't let him down. My determination increased when I learned that he was planning to bring the production to Broadway."

Brynner perfected his lines with the aid of a guitar. "The school had a recording of *Twelfth Night*," he said. "I played it over and over. Then I transmitted every sound to my guitar. Each inflection, tone, intensity, and syllable. I was finally tone perfect.

"True, the part of Fabian the servant was small. But I was sure that I'd be noticed. Was I wrong! Opening night was on December 8, 1941, the day after the bombing of Pearl Harbor. I bombed too."

Yul tried to enlist in the army, but again his circus injuries kept him out. "I thought I might have better luck in another city," he said, "so I took a train to Washington. I had heard they were so desperate for volunteers that they took anyone with two legs and two arms. But it was the same thing. I was rejected. In disgust I took a job with the Office of War Information as a French-speaking announcer."

His section was charged with disseminating French propaganda. "Too often," he said, "they would run out of suitable material and repeat themselves." For a change of pace, Brynner rewrote some of the prepared messages. Occasionally, he fooled the censors. The three he liked best were:

The true Frenchman is loved by everybody. And he in turn loves everybody. Especially the ladies.

Henry LaFava should be awarded the Croix de Guerre *for his croissants. All of our brave soldiers deserve them.*

The quickest way to end this war is by transporting gossips

*to the front lines, where they could talk the enemy to
death.*

Several of Yul's contributions came to the attention of
congressional critics who felt the government allotment to
the OWI was much too large. Elmer Davis, then in charge
of the agency, frequently had to go to Capitol Hill to offer
apologies. "Until I met Yul in person," Davis said, "I thought
he was just another wiseacre. But it was very apparent that
this young man had depth and talent. However, I couldn't
stop wondering why he felt it necessary to so dramatically
keep himself in the forefront."

Brynner's impeccable French made him a valuable OWI
employee. "But that wasn't the only reason," said Robert
Jackson, a retired high school teacher who occupied the
desk next to him. "He was often asked to help out in other
sections because of his language fluency. I asked him how
he had picked up so many foreign tongues. His answers
rarely were the same; however, I always found them entertaining. In the year I worked with him he told me that he
had been a child prodigy at the Sorbonne; he had once served
as a cabin boy on a ship that was manned by a miniature
League of Nations; his father had been a traveling mis-
sionary; each of his mistresses had come from a different
country."

Jackson said that he was never certain how Brynner had
acquired his language facility. He guessed that Yul had a
sharp ear and the moment he heard a strange language, he
was able to mimic it perfectly. "But he had one language
hangup," said Jackson. "For some reason he couldn't master
English. He realized that his accent was still very noticeable.
He'd try the strangest remedies to fix it. One of them was
to sit on the floor pigeon-toed reading aloud detective pulp
magazines. Whenever there'd be a break in our work, he'd
pull one out. 'The heroes and villains in these stories,' he'd

say, 'speak the real kind of American English. They are my teachers.' "

During Yul's employment at the OWI, his mother became ill. Doctors said she was suffering from a rare form of leukemia. They recommended hospitalization. The moment Brynner learned about the diagnosis he began investigating treatments. When he was satisfied that the New York Presbyterian Medical Center was the best place for an adult with that disease, he checked her in.

There are conflicting stories about Maria's arrival in the United States. Her son told several reporters that he had sent for her in 1941 after winning a great deal of money in a week-long poker game. To some others he said that his mother and sister left France at the same time he did. He once claimed that she had been brought over by an American used-car dealer who had a large open-air lot in Troy, New York. He had seen her picture and was intrigued with it. Whichever version is correct, it is certain that Yul was extremely devoted to his mother.

"Her illness really threw him," said Vera. "Never before had I seen him so devastated. To help pay for her medical expenses he took on a series of part-time jobs. He sang in some unsavory nightclubs, entertained at parties. Even parked cars. He made sure that our mother had the best room, best doctors, and around-the-clock nurses."

One of the nurses, Beatrice DiCello, recalled his grief. "He'd sit by her side for hours," she said. "Although sometimes he'd confuse me by referring to her as his grandmother. He'd read everything he could find on adult leukemia. Then he'd show the article to the doctor. Once, when he was told the suggested cure was a lot of quack nonsense, he shouted, 'If quack nonsense can save her, then I suggest we try it!' He never had a chance to find out. She died the next day."

After his mother's death, Yul lost interest in working for the OWI. A friend told him that CBS was hiring for tel-

evision, then in its infancy. "They needed a master of ceremonies for a variety show called *Mr. Jones and His Neighbors*,"
Yul said. "Several dozen others showed up for the audition.
I was chosen." Brynner chuckled as he added, "Because of
my head size. In addition to interviewing the guests and
singing, the MC was required to model comic hats. They had
already been purchased, and they were extra large. Fortunately, I have a big head."

The show had six performances. "It was a disaster," Yul
recalled. "But nobody complained. You have to remember
that this was in the early forties and there were damn few
people watching the show. At the time there were less than
five thousand sets in the entire country. Pictures were fuzzy.
We didn't dare take advertising, not that anyone in their
right mind would give us any. Our only interruptions were
station breaks, and there were plenty of them. During each
show the sound track would fail. The engineer would try to
restore it. When he finally got it going, everyone sounded
like Mickey Mouse."

After *Mr. Jones and His Neighbors* folded, Brynner was
assigned to help out on a wrestling show. He was disgusted
by the apparent phoniness. "Realism is what we want!" he
shouted as he charged into one of the surprised contestants
and tossed him to the floor.

"Yul's boss quickly realized that he wasn't the best person to assist with wrestling matches. He was given another
chance and told to furnish weather reports. Not only was he
required to announce the weather information, but also to
research it—from the synoptic in *The New York Times*. All
went well until he became bored again. Excitedly, he announced that viewers were in for a gigantic snowstorm. This
was in the middle of July.

"We wondered why he wasn't fired," said Paula Mos-
ley, a former CBS switchboard operator. "We figured that
he knew where the body was buried. But all kidding aside,

he was kept for one reason only—it was very obvious that he had oodles of talent."

Chekhov continuously warned his former student that the "picture radio" wouldn't last very long. "He would ridicule the things I had to do," Yul said. " 'For this I taught you?' he'd say unhappily. I'd tell him that I was willing to compromise myself for the $100 weekly salary they paid me. That didn't make him any happier. I'd try to reassure him that I was merely using television as a stepping-stone. Broadway was still my aim. However, he seemed so downcast that I handed in my notice to quit."

Yul was out of work when he met wife number one. "I kept urging my agent, Margaret Lindley, to find me a suitable stage role," he said. "She told me that the only available parts called for actors who spoke accent-free English. Instead she gave me some frank advice: 'Meet a nice American girl who can help you improve your speech.' "

Before he had a chance to reply she shuffled through her client list and decided on Virginia Gilmore, a twenty-four-year-old actress whom Samuel Goldwyn had called, "An honest-to-God American beauty with brains who even writes poems."

Virginia, the daughter of British parents, was born in El Monte, California. Her original name was Sherman Poole. She had been educated at the Immaculate Heart Convent in Hollywood, San Mateo Junior College, and the University of California. Although she often played secondary roles, she had impressive screen credits: *Winter Carnival*, *Jennie*, *The Westerner*, *Laddie*, *Western Union*, *Tall, Dark and Handsome*, *Berlin Correspondent*, *The Pride of the Yankees*.

When Yul met her she was on location in New York. Lindley invited both of them to a party she was giving. Usually, Brynner was garrulous around the ladies, but on this occasion he was very subdued. "I was too busy staring at her legs to do anything else," he said. "I had just been told that the American Physical Foundation had selected her as the female possessing the 'prettiest and healthiest legs in the country.' "

He was further enchanted when Virginia started discussing politics and social conditions. "I thought I wouldn't take on a wife for at least a dozen years," he said. "Was I wrong! Not only did she look good but sounded good."

They dated steadily for five weeks. During that time he learned that she was probably the only girl in Hollywood who didn't dance or know how to swing a tennis racquet. Instead, she swam, skied, and read thick books that she seemed to understand. A brief note in Louella Parsons' column announced the wedding: "Virginia Gilmore and some gypsy she met in New York will be married on September 6, 1943."

"Right off," Virginia said, "I learned that my husband-to-be was out of the ordinary. I had to return to California, and Yul was still in New York. He had to take a milk train to get to the Coast. It took five days. Remember, this was during the war. He was so impatient—not just because he was coming out for our wedding, but because he was naturally restless. Every time the train stopped to load, he'd insist on helping the railroad crew speed things up. Then he began giving signals for the train to depart. By the time it reached California, he was practically running the train. So much so that a conducter said to me, 'Lady, what will we do now that our boss is leaving?' "

Brynner took his forthcoming marriage very seriously. "I had loved before," he said. "Perhaps a dozen times, but never in this way. I was determined that Virginia and I would have an excellent marriage. After all, I am basically a family man."

—CHAPTER THREE—

Stage
Versus
Television

YUL kept telling his new wife that the legitimate theater was far superior to Hollywood. Virginia, who was being heralded as a fast-rising screen star, tried to refute his arguments. She failed. "Nobody ever succeeded in convincing him that he was wrong," she said. Reluctantly, she agreed to move east, where they rented a small, walk-up apartment in lower Manhattan.

Often they didn't know where their next meal was coming from. "We didn't have any savings, and our unemployment insurance had expired," said Virginia. "We were delighted to be invited out because it meant getting a free meal. However, it had a serious drawback. We'd stuff ourselves silly and get sick at our stomachs after not having eaten properly for days."

The morning after these food hangovers, Brynner would pace the floor of their tiny kitchen, swallow a bicarbonate of soda, and promise his wife that eating that way would soon be unnecessary. "He had no doubts that he was going to be successful," she said. "If ever a man had complete faith in his ability, it was my husband."

When things got very bleak, Yul would borrow money from his sister, Vera, who was gaining fame as a lyric opera soprano. But it didn't help much. Money in hand, he'd invite acquaintances and neighbors to the nearest restaurant. He'd always pick up the check, but insist on being allowed to sit at the head of the table and coerce his guests into ordering the same things he did.

During this impoverished period Yul kept making the rounds of all casting calls. When his turn came to read, he would patronizingly announce how the role should be played. "It was the manner in which he said it that irritated me," said Frank Loehman, a former casting director. "There always were fireworks when I'd turn him down. It wasn't a case of his simply being arrogant—I don't think he knew any other way.

"A typical example of what I mean happened when we were casting for a college professor. Yul was at the theater promptly when the doors opened. I handed him the script and told him to read some lines. So what does he do? Looks at it scornfully. 'That's not the way a genuine professor talks!' he yelled as he tossed the script down. Then he proceeded to give me his own version."

Finally, Brynner managed to land a very minor role in *The Moon Vine*, a period comedy about the Deep South. His characterization of a southern gentleman was hardly convincing. The only mention he received was a review in the *New York Sun*: "Among the cast members are . . . Youl Bryner [he still went by that name] whose southern accent is as believable as hominy served to an Eskimo."

"That notice really upset me," Yul recalled. "Will Geer was also in that play. He couldn't help noticing my low spirits. He told me that before an actor can succeed he had to suffer a failure. 'This is yours,' he said. Looking back, I suppose it made sense, but at the time it didn't help much. What really helped is that the play had a very brief run. As soon as it closed I forgot all about it."

Yul's belief in his ability quickly returned. Virginia recalled that several days after *The Moon Vine* folded, she and her husband went to a movie that John Barrymore was in. "On the way out of the cinema," she said, "a woman walking alongside of us remarked to her companion that Barrymore was probably the finest actor in the world. Yul turned and bowed. 'No, madam,' he said. 'I am!' He wasn't being flip —he really meant it."

Ludmilla Pitoeff, his former drama teacher, was opening in *The House In Paris*, which was being premiered in Toronto. She recommended her former pupil for one of the roles. "We gave him one," said Marvin Marcus, the show's assistant producer. "That was our biggest mistake. Ludmilla kept telling him that he deserved much better lines. That with his background and training, his name should be in bigger letters. It didn't require much telling to convince him. Every day without fail, I could anticipate fresh demands from a very angry Mongol-French-Chinese actor."

The play was having financial problems, and the producers tried to attract new backers. One of them berated Yul's second-act entrance. Brynner walked over to the man, lifted him up, and hurled him into the orchestra pit. "Needless to say," Marcus recalled, "I had to tell Brynner he was through. But even then it wasn't the usual firing. As soon as I opened my mouth to speak, he beat me to it. 'I quit!' he shouted. 'I won't tolerate any money man telling me how to perform!' "

When Yul returned to New York after his brief stay with *The House In Paris*, he and Virginia were once again insolvent. "Nothing was left from the money he had earned," his wife said. "Innocently, I suggested that perhaps he should consider returning to CBS. He reacted violently and began throwing the furniture around."

Gertrude Malloy, a former beautician, lived next door. "Those two were always at it," she said. "But minutes later they were lovey dovey. Before either left they'd stand in the hallway and smooch as if they planned to be apart for months.

It was exactly the same way when they returned. Even if it was only a short time later. More hugging and more kissing."

Virginia had repeated telephone calls from the West Coast offering her assorted roles. Yul made her turn them down. "You don't want to be the queen of B pictures," he'd say.

Finally, she signed a contract to play a leading role in the Broadway production of *Dear Ruth*, a comedy by Norman Krasna. She managed to get an advance on her salary. The Brynners celebrated on imported caviar and vintage champagne. The play was a hit and ran for more than two years. Gilmore was singled out for giving an outstanding performance.

Yul claimed that he didn't resent his wife's success, but when he had too much to drink he'd say morosely, "I'm beginning to think it doesn't matter how good you are but how lucky you are!"

While Virginia was appearing in *Dear Ruth*, he took a job at the Blue Angel, a New York nightclub. "I was their featured attraction," he said. "Regardless of my picture being plastered all over the place, the employees usually outnumbered the customers. But I tried not to let it bother me. I kept telling myself that I was good. I suppose that's all that really matters. Once you allow yourself to think differently, you may as well toss in the towel."

Brynner's first break on Broadway came early in 1946. He was selected to play opposite Mary Martin in *Lute Song*, a musical fantasy. Michael Myerberg, the show's producer, recalled Yul's audition. "My guess is that he really came to the audition seeking one of the secondary roles," Myerberg said. "He looked so dejected that I actually felt sorry for him. But that wasn't the reason why he was selected. I did it because I believed that he was an excellent actor. Mary Martin had told me that he'd be superb for the part of Tsai-Yong. She had seen him perform. When I told him that he was getting the leading male role, I don't think he believed me until we held our first rehearsal."

John Houseman, who directed *Lute Song*, said, "Michael had come up with this dynamic, strangely beautiful young man of Russian-Chinese origin. I remembered him vaguely as a sporadic announcer in the French section of the OWI. His voice was untrained and had a wavering pitch. But he satisfied all the other requirements—a sexy, exotic leading man with interesting speech and a vaguely Oriental look."

Brynner had seen the play when he was a young boy living in China. *Lute Song* had been adapted by Sidney Howard and Will Irwin from a 500-year-old Chinese classic called *Pi-Pi-Ki*. It was about a provincial scholar, Tsai-Yong [played by Yul Brynner, using the new spelling of his name for the first time], who lives in the village of Tchinlieou. He leaves his parents in care of his wife, Tchao-ou-Niang [Mary Martin] to seek his fortune in the big city. At the time, a person's worth was determined by the number of books he had read. Since Tsai-Yong had pored through 6,000 volumes, he is made the chief magistrate. But in order to receive this great honor he must take on a second wife—the reigning prince's daughter. He does.

Years later he learns that his parents died during a famine and that his faithful first wife sold her hair to pay for their burial. She, too, is starving and has been reduced to begging. Tsai-Yong realizes the error of his ways and decides to return.

Although Yul had the awkward assignment of portraying the errant son and husband who finds himself married to the boss's daughter, the reviewers called his performance, "Honest . . . Restrained . . . Natural."

"We had a superior cast," Yul said. "Besides Mary Martin, one of the theater greats, *Lute Song* had Nancy Davis, now Nancy Reagan. If Nancy had stuck to the theater, I believe she'd have developed into a first-rate star—which may be as good as being First Lady."

Molly Picon, the Yiddish matinee idol, saw *Lute Song* and was so carried away with Yul's performance that she went backstage to compliment him. She told him how much she had enjoyed the show. He responded in Yiddish that he was delighted that a busy lady like herself took time out to visit him. When she asked him how he happened to speak Yiddish, he said that his great-grandmother was Jewish and that she was now living in Israel.

"I knew he was pulling my leg," Picon said. "But it was his way of making me feel welcome. He was still in costume when he walked me back to my car. That was when a young lady handed him a program to sign. Suddenly, his whole manner changed. He ignored her as well as me. Without saying a word he ran back to his dressing room."

The previous day an incident had occurred that made Brynner apprehensive of autograph-seekers. As he was about to get into his taxi, a middle-aged woman asked him to sign her program. "She wanted me to write, 'To Lizzie with love'," Yul said. "After obliging her, a couple of other autograph-seekers thrust out their programs. I was busy signing them when this powerfully built man came charging over, shouting and waving his fists. The Lizzie whose program I had signed was this man's wife. He thought I was her secret lover. A policeman managed to quiet him down, while another policeman escorted me to my taxi. Ever since then I've become very cautious about writing personal messages."

The picture editor of *Collier's* was so impressed with the lavish costumes worn by the cast that he decided to run a large spread of *Lute Song*, reproducing several of the scenes in color. McKay Norris, who played Prince Nineou, the Imperial Preceptor, was enraged when his name was omitted from the captions. "Despite my being decked out in the show's most elegant robe, I'm not identified!" he shouted. He blamed Brynner for the foul-up and kept calling him a Judas who cared only for self-aggrandizement. Yul insisted that art meant more to him than fame and wealth. He tried to prove it at the next day's matinee when he stood back and allowed Norris to take the last bow. He also sent the infuriated actor a silver cigarette case, which he could ill afford. Grandiose gestures were Yul's stock in trade.

Although Brynner professed to care little about money, he used his new prosperity to acquire the services of a professional dresser. He hired Don Lawson to help him with the makeup and to assist him backstage. "Some of the clothes that Mr. B. had to wear," said Lawson, "were so intricate, I almost had to pour him into them. He'd scream, but long ago I learned that it never meant anything. Many unkind things have been written about him. How hard he is to work with. How he's a self-calculating liar. How he cares only about himself."

Lawson, who worked for Brynner for more than a dozen years, insisted that he found these accusations untrue. "Oh, he'd snap at me at times," he recalled, "but there always seemed to be a good reason. He saved his real anger for the higher-ups. As for his telling fairy tales, he always did it with tongue in cheek. The newspapers wanted something dramatic, and Mr. B. wasn't about to disappoint them. They begged to be deceived."

In the year-long tour that followed the five-month Broadway run, *Lute Song* played well to audiences sentimental about Mary Martin and intrigued by the new, lively image of Yul Brynner. He handed out interviews left and right; some were pure fiction, some contained selective truth, some were insultingly honest.

"American theater-goers in the sticks! Eighth-grade, dressed-up clots with their brains in the aisle!" (Los Angeles)

"My gypsy mother gave birth to me when the pony she was riding stumbled in a blinding snowstorm." (Chicago)

"Kansas City is where you can't kid anybody!" (Kansas City)

One story that boomeranged was the fanciful tale Yul told about having served in Spain with the International Brigade. When a persevering reporter confronted him with unshakable evidence that he had never even been to that country, Brynner said, "I planned to go, but I got sick. Doesn't that count for anything? The trouble with the world today is that it has become too exact-fact conscious!" After that encounter, however, he eliminated the reference to Spain from his show-bill biography.

Several weeks later it surfaced again when Vince Hartnett, a vigorous anti-Communist spokesman, charged him with having been anti-Franco, and associating with well-known left-wingers. Yul dismissed the attack. His only comment was, "I bet even left-wingers are occasionally good to their mothers."

Several weeks after *Lute Song* closed, Virginia learned that she was pregnant. She stayed in New York with a friend, actress Haila Stoddard, while Yul traveled to England to appear in *Dark Eyes*, a musical comedy about a group of expatriate Russians who are houseguests in an upper-class Western home. A London theater critic lauded his performance, but voiced some puzzlement. "I know that Brynner isn't a birthright Yank," he said. "But for the life of me I can't decide what he is. To me, he remains a deep mystery."

Yul, who often sent notes to reviewers, replied: "Life would be dull indeed if we didn't have some mystery. In my own way I try to provide some."

For five months he continued to perplex the patrons of *Dark Eyes*, beginning with his entrance in the play's first scene. Although his role called for instant chatter, he'd stand very still and say nothing. After about thirty seconds he'd finally speak. The bewildered audience would applaud this strange ploy. Brynner felt he had a rational explanation for his behavior. "Professor Chekhov once told me that British audiences needed time to settle down," he said. "I am simply giving them that opportunity."

The night after he gave his final performance he made a fast trip to New York, but returned to Europe several days later to appear in a Paris nightclub. Pierre Durand, the owner, had met Yul at a party. "He had a great deal to drink that night," Durand recalled. "He challenged everyone to do pushups. After he beat us all, he entertained us with some of his gypsy songs. On the spot I offered him a job. He accepted.

"Yul was very good for business. The place would be packed when he was there. His routine rarely varied. He'd bum a cigarette from me before he'd go out. Then the lights would be turned down low. The drummer would bang his cymbals. *Voilà.* Yul would jump out wearing a tight-fitting Russian blouse and tight-fitting black satin trousers. He'd dangle the cigarette from the corner of his mouth and glower at the audience. Then he'd sit on the bare floor and start to sing. At first you could hardly hear him; then he'd get louder and louder. Although he did the same routine every night, the same people would come back to listen to him sing those haunting melodies. I was sorry to see him leave. Not just because he brought in customers, but I really liked him. He told me he had to go home to diaper his brand-new son."

Virginia had given birth to a baby boy. Yul was elated. He did everything young fathers are supposed to. Even passed out cigars. The infant was named Yul, Jr., but Brynner insisted that the child be called Rocky because he looked so strong and already had a firm grip.

Shortly after the baby's arrival, NBC television offered his parents a half-hour Mr. and Mrs. show. "For thirteen weeks we had a ball," Brynner said. "The two of us were the producers, writers, directors, and performers. We were supposed to be sitting in our living room, chatting. Suddenly, Virginia would look surprised and say, 'We're on the air.' Some top-level genius had thought up that clever introduction. But no one bothered us. Anything we did was permissible, as long as we didn't say 'damn!'

"Occasionally, we had guests if we could hoodwink some unsuspecting celebrity into showing up. We paid their taxi fare. The budget didn't allow for any more. But despite that we managed to have some colorful moments. Once we staged a meeting between the artist Salvador Dali and cartoonist Al Capp, whose *Li'l Abner* strip was extremely popular. The conversation between Dali and Capp was so censorable, I was amazed we were allowed to stay on the air—I suppose the reason was that they didn't say 'damn.' But they tossed around many more vigorous four-letter words. In the end they did something that was very charming. They both drew on the same sheet of paper. It was during Al's Shmoo period and he did a sketch of that strange squashlike creature. When he finished, Dali put a window in the Shmoo's stomach, showing a desert horizon and skeletons in the distance."

At the end of the show's thirteen weeks, Yul was rehired by CBS. "We realized that he was a brilliant television director," said Martin Ritt, a CBS producer. "Probably the best we ever had. Every one of his programs had his special stamp on it. His innovations were so unique that the BBC sent two of their top men to study them."

Among the programs Yul directed were *Studio One, Omnibus, The Robert Q. Lewis Show, Danger, The Stork Club Show,* and *Life With Snarky Parker,* which featured the Baird marionettes. "I had learned that good television called for lots of ingenuity," Yul said. "And I always had plenty of that commodity. In that business surprise is very necessary. To get it you have to scream, torture, and practically commit mayhem." At rehearsals he would bring a baseball and toss it around. "They would never know who was going to get it next," said Yul. "I found it to be an excellent method of keeping everybody alert."

He also had a major hand in other programs. "I telecast the first walkout the Russians staged at the United Nations," he said. "At the time no editorial comment was allowed. I was accused of allowing my camera to dwell much too long on empty chairs—this being the equivalent of an editorial. It was so dramatic that it made the front pages of more than a dozen newspapers!"

Serious clashes between Yul and management occurred daily. On one occasion, distracted by noise in the control room, he thundered, "Who is responsible for that bloody racket?" When told that it was a prospective sponsor, he refused to apologize. "I will not continue until that idiot leaves!" he yelled. The would-be sponsor left.

Another time, a new CBS executive passed him a note criticizing a performance. "Who is that creep?" roared Yul. When a terrified aide told him that the man was a vice president, Brynner became angrier still. "Get him out of here!" he ordered. "I detest anything concerned with vice!"

Brynner was well known for his ability to swear in many foreign languages. Once, under the pressure of hammering out a segment of *Studio One*, he began using obscene words in French. An executive's wife who understood the language overheard his blast and reported the incident to her husband. Yul was asked to apologize. Instead, he quit. He was rehired shortly after the lady left the building. Some of the other layoffs were of longer duration. One of the dismissals lasted several months. He used that period to make his first motion picture.

He had thought that *Lute Song* would be his introduction to the movies. "Judy Garland was interested in doing it," he said. "She suggested that I be her costar. I was given a screen test, but never got to be Tsai-Yong in a movie. When Lazlo Bendek, a Hollywood director, saw the test, he selected me to appear in *Port of New York*, a B picture he was making for Eagle-Lion. I'm being kind when I classify it as a class B movie. It was class Z!"

Yul was cast as a suave and sinister-looking gangster who is head of a powerful dope ring that wants to hijack a ship carrying medical supplies. He plans to substitute sand in place of the valuable cargo so that the customs inspectors won't be suspicious.

"The movie was so bad," Yul said, "that when I was finally caught the audience whistled and cheered."

Critics, like the audiences, panned the movie but they hailed the photography. Brynner, never one to know his place, had elbowed his way in behind the camera and gave the film a fresh documentary quality.

As soon as the film was completed, Brynner returned to CBS, where he continued to harass the top brass. "They kept him for only one reason," said Sidney Lumet, who was Yul's assistant. "And that was because they knew he was good."

Abe Burrows, recalling the *Stork Club Show*, said, "Right off, he thought something dramatic had to be done to save that production. More than $100,000 had been spent on the set, but he felt something was lacking. He decided the pop of champagne corks should start things off so he stationed dozens of waiters all around the room, armed with magnums of champagne. Then with split-second precision they all popped the corks. Yul moved the camera in to catch shots of the resulting foam. It was sheer genius. But I had to stop him from wanting to wade in and lap up the spilled champagne. 'Such a waste!' he kept muttering."

Cora Baird, cohost of the *Life With Snarky Parker* show, was another of his television fans. She said, "He had the ability to excite us and make us like what we were doing.

The results were always spectacular. There was a spirit of gaiety on the set. He even made our marionettes laugh."

Brynner once told Walter Bankoff, a writer attached to the *Robert Q. Lewis Show*, "CBS pays me a thousand dollars a week because they know I'm an expert director. I plan to continue doing it for years."

"Granted, with him nothing was ever certain," said Bankoff. I'm sure that he intended to remain for a long time. But soon he left to appear in *The King and I*. His life was never the same."

CHAPTER FOUR

Every
Inch
A King

THERE are numerous accounts of how Brynner came to the attention of Richard Rodgers and Oscar Hammerstein, composer and author of *The King and I*. Mary Martin, Marlene Dietrich, Noël Coward, and Rex Harrison all claimed credit for Yul's eventual triumph. Mary Martin's persistence was the chief factor. Having appeared with him in *Lute Song*, she was convinced that he would make an ideal King Mongkut of Siam.

"In the late forties, I heard that Oscar and Dick were looking for a male lead for their new show," she recalled. "I felt that no one could play the part but Yul Brynner—it seemed that the historical role had been written especially for him. But when I tried to tell this to him, he said that he was much too busy to appear in some fool musical. No amount of coaxing helped. I appealed to his wife. Together we nagged."

"Those two ganged up on me," Brynner said. "Mary and Virginia plotted to persuade me to change my mind. I was earning good money as a television director and wasn't in need of a switch. For three and a half months I wouldn't answer calls from John Fearley, the show's casting director. I was fed up with acting. The roles I had until then I had not enjoyed. But they refused to give up and kept pounding away. Reluctantly, I agreed to audition."

Richard Rodgers relished telling how Brynner was first brought to his attention. "Over the years it became one of my favorite stories," he said. "Rex Harrison was one of the actors we considered. We got in touch with him, but we couldn't come to terms. There were other candidates. Oscar and I wanted Alfred Drake, who was then the biggest male star in the musical theater. We tried to convince him to undertake the role. He told us that he was too busy with other projects. Discouraged, Oscar and I went to another round of what had become wearisome auditions.

"Johnny Fearley was casting for us. He nodded as we came in. He asked if we were ready for the next contestant. We told him to go ahead. Out came a partially baldheaded, muscular fellow with a bony, oriental-like face. He scowled at us, then sat down cross-legged tailor fashion in the middle of the stage."

Brynner plunked a few whacking, angry chords on the battered guitar he carried, glared around, and broke out in a plaintive high-pitched wail. The sound was like the crash of thin, expensive glass. The syllables he sang were dimly Asiatic, untranslatable—Yul admitted that he had made them up as he went along. But to Rodgers and Hammerstein they clearly told the tale of an autocratic monarch up against an exasperating, unfathomable smother of starched English petticoats. And the sounds ended with a tender laugh. Oscar and Richard looked at each other—here was the king they had been seeking.

"You're really in tune with the character," he was told.

"What character?" Brynner asked.

The King and I had been adapted from the book *Anna and the King of Siam*, written by Margaret Landon. It concerned the adventures of Anna Leonowens, a Welsh governess who brought her young son to the half-barbarous Far Eastern monarchy of what is now Thailand. It was ruled by an arrogant, despotic emperor. Her assignment was to teach his sixty-seven children basic English—reading and writing. She also made them aware of good manners and dancing. Then she started on the king.

At first the fierce-looking monarch screamed and stormed. Slowly, he too became a willing student. He was made aware of the outside world by the "scientific foreigner." Though the two clashed bitterly, they learned to respect one another. Unlike most Broadway musicals of the time, this one didn't have the usual love story. The king's relationship with Anna was platonic. They never exchanged a kiss, yet their involvement was more powerful than anything carnal could have been.

"Don't read *Anna and the King of Siam*," Yul was instructed. "We don't want you to get all mixed up. It will only distract things. We want you to feel, to develop the traits of the king as they are shaped in the script."

The ink was scarcely dry on the contract before Yul was at Brentano's, an elegant Manhattan bookstore. He bought two copies of the Landon book. "In case I lose one," he told Virginia. Brynner stayed up all that night, reading and making notes. The pertinent jottings were reproduced later in several newspapers:

"Ah, it is 1862. Now, I know when I am."

"The King is fifty-nine years old. Well, a young fifty-nine. He was short and skinny. Should I lose weight, become gaunt?"

"The King turns purple with rage and howls when he gets angry. That's easy. So do I."

"The King loves children. So do I."

"The King ate simple food, mostly boiled rice. Ugh! We did that when we were very poor."

"If the King admired a woman, he was apt to show it by pouring a bottle of rose water over her head. Wonder how Virginia would go for that?"

Yul was dreadfully upset by the king's cruelties. The following morning he took the book and himself to Rodgers' office.

"King Mongkut was not a nice man," he said, shaking his head. "An interesting man but quite horrible. What's entertaining about him? He gives me the cold shudders. He put his wives in dungeons. He deprived people of their fingernails. Is this entertainment?"

"You were told not to read the book," Rodgers said irritably. "I assure you, he's quite a different person in the show."

"So I play an historical distortion," said Yul.

"That's about it."

"Well, we'll see how it goes."

Brynner had only agreed to sign an eight-month contract. He was careful to negotiate a leave of absence from CBS television. "Directing is what I really do," he said. Even after the show was in rehearsal, he went to CBS on his days off. "Checking up on the company," he explained. It was no small role to be cast in the lead of a Rodgers and Hammerstein play, yet at the start he was diffident, almost insultingly offhand about the musical. The only person he seemed in awe of was his costar Gertrude Lawrence. But even in her case he often felt it necessary to appear to be truculent.

An intercom linked their dressing rooms. They kept up a steady conversation while applying makeup. But she could only speak to Yul when he pressed down his button. He could hear everything that was going on while she put on her costume. "That's quite proper," he said. "After all, shouldn't the king have the master switch?"

During rehearsals, Irene Sharaff, the show's chief costume designer, noticed Brynner's hairline was fast disappearing. She recommended that he shave his entire head. "It will look more romantic," she tried to convince him.

"I thought her advice was a bunch of nonsense," he said, "but she kept at it. Finally, in New Haven, I agreed to shave it all off." He added begrudgingly, "I suppose it was a good idea." He often told reporters that by shaving his head he had saved the sex image of millions of bald men.

"The effect was instantly sensational," said Don Lawson, Yul's dresser. "He looked at himself in the mirror. Evidently, he liked what he saw. I was instructed to keep it that way."

Lawson used poodle clippers to rid his boss of five-o'clock shadow on his head. To make him look brownish yellow, he daubed him with furniture polish. When it blotched in New Haven, bringing out red rings, walnut juice was substituted. It was applied to Brynner's skull, ears, and chest, down to his waist. In some of the scenes he wore diaper-like pants which exposed his legs, which were also tinted.

Yul toyed with the idea of taking injections of melanin to give his skin the desired shade. His doctors vetoed the scheme. He thought of swallowing atabrine, a malaria repressant, which has a tendency to turn the body yellow. The doctors disapproved of that also.

"Mr. B. insisted on being allowed to handle the facial makeup by himself," Lawson said. "He would draw ferocious-looking eyebrows. Then make the bones of his face stand out by rubbing in a little of the walnut juice above his eyes. He'd add years to his age by etching in dark lines alongside his nostrils."

When Brynner felt the transformation was just right, he'd march into Lawrence's dressing room. She would examine him closely as he pirouetted around. If she approved, she'd curtsy and say, "Master, you are brewed to perfection."

One afternoon, he and Gertrude were on their way to the theater when they encountered an accident. A young boy, chasing a soccer ball, had been hit by an automobile.

Brynner sprang to where the child lay sprawled and yelled, "Police! Ambulance! Etcetera!" Yul had adopted the king's impatience with English and had taken to bellowing "Etcetera!" Several bystanders took the actor literally and called the fire department and a local Roman Catholic priest. "Fortunately, the boy was only grazed," Gertrude Lawrence said later. "I'm sure that a few more of Yul's etceteras would have brought the nearest school principal and an army captain!"

When the play opened in Boston it was too long. It was cut radically and became much too short. After hurried changes it was put in its final form. Almost as an afterthought, a song left over from *South Pacific* was added. It was *Getting to Know You*. It had been shelved because it was felt that it would be too tentative to express the reckless love affair of the nurse and the Frenchman in *South Pacific*, but it was just right for Rodgers and Hammerstein's new show. Recordings by Sinatra and Crosby were grooved and on the street in forty-eight hours.

With very pertinent knowledge, Brynner convinced Rodgers and Hammerstein to toss out some of the spoken dialogue. "Oriental languages," he explained, "do not use article adjectives. It is not their ignorance of English—it is their disdain for it. Knock out the " 'an,' 'a,' 'the,' and the like!" A bemused Gertrude Lawrence went around saying, "Here soap. Wash face."

Although her name appeared above his on the marquee and program, he didn't make any fuss about it. "She was the only person I'd let get away with it," he said. "I truly adored her. Everything that woman did was magnificent. She was a true professional. Perhaps that's why we were so compatible. We both demanded integrity. Gossip columnists reported that we were feuding. Nonsense! We had a routine that we used to repeat before each act. I would kiss her passionately, and she would say, 'Don't be long darling.'

Then we would be ready to face the audience. Does that sound like two people who are quarreling?"

Yul said the only real argument they ever had was over a cablegram he'd received from Rex Harrison on opening night. Harrison had played the king in the screen's *Anna and the King of Siam*. About an hour before the curtain went up, he sent Yul a wire: "The King is dead! Long live the King!"

"For some absurd reason, Gertie wanted me to tack it to the wall. I wanted to file it away. The more we disagreed, the more we argued. We went at it like two howling hyenas. Naturally, she won. But on the next day, to demonstrate there weren't any hard feelings, she gave me a present that I shall always cherish. It's a wooden fish. On the back she had scrawled, 'To the catch of the season. Mrs. Anna Siam, 1951–19?' "

The first date marked the opening curtain at the St. James Theater, March 29, 1951. Young people today may find it difficult to realize the impact the show had at that time. "Musicals and leading men will never be the same after last night," said Otis L. Gurney of the New York *Herald Tribune*. "Brynner set an example that will be hard to follow . . . Probably the best show of the decade."

Other critics called Yul's performance "Outstanding . . . Remarkable . . . Truly magnificent." Brooks Atkinson of *The New York Times*, although equally enthusiastic, wrote, "Mr. Brynner may not be the world's greatest singer, but he makes his way safely."

Instead of being elated by all the glowing reviews, Yul was displeased by the negative reference to his singing. In the show he did not use his natural singing voice, which he described as a *basso-cantanto*. "I don't believe the audience realized I didn't actually vocalize," he said. "I sort of talked my solo number: *Is A Puzzlement*. In rehearsal I sang it, but quickly discovered that it was out of character and began using a speaking-singing version. It seemed right and I stayed with it, even if it was thought to be delivered in a rather flat tone. Everybody except *The New York Times* loved it."

He wasn't being completely accurate. Several nights later when Yul finished his song, a man sitting in the front row started making razzing sounds. "I felt he badly needed to be taught proper respect," Brynner recalled. "I stopped what I was doing and said, 'Sir, you are interrupting the show. You are disturbing the audience.' It got tremendous applause. And the troublemaker was clobbered by the lady sitting behind him."

Brynner's defiance disappeared the moment he was surrounded by children. "It wasn't any pretense," Lawson said. "They knew he loved them and they loved him back."

Occasionally, a negative event spotlights a segment of a person's character. Once when Yul was backstage, a bearded priest approached him for a contribution. Instead of sending for his wallet, the shocked cast watched him strike the frocked clergyman. Later, he explained his reason. "That man was no more a priest than I'm a saint," he said. "I had seen a picture of him in the morning paper. Not only had he falsely donned a priest's habit and solicited money for a phony charity, but he had sexually molested a four-year-old girl. If there's anything that sets me off it is when someone is cruel to a child!"

Throughout the run of *The King and I*, Brynner conducted acting classes for the children in the cast. They'd sit around in a circle as he instructed them how to speak, how to dress, how to walk, how to posture. "I wouldn't call it teaching," Yul protested. "It was more the other way 'round. I'm convinced that children contribute a lot more to adults than they get from them. But still we have to remember that children are children."

He said that his biggest problem with them occurred in

the second act when he had ten minutes of steady dialogue. "They were required to sit very still while I pontificated," he recalled. "Once, one of the boys started fidgeting. He distracted me so much that I missed a cue. I finally had to pick him up and spank him right on the stage. The audience thought it was part of the play and began to applaud. As soon as the curtain came down the boy came over to me. 'Mr. Brynner,' he said proudly, 'don't you think I got a real big hand?' I should have spanked him again. Instead, I just laughed and hugged him."

On another occasion Yul was in the midst of his death scene whispering final instructions to Anna and his prime minister when he noticed one of the youngsters fast asleep. "Not only that," he said, "but he looked as if he was about to topple into the orchestra pit. I raised my voice, hoping to wake him up, but I didn't have any luck. We had played a matinee earlier in the day and he was really tired. By now he had one foot hanging over the edge of the stage. I couldn't get off my deathbed to stop him. Somehow, I managed to call it to the attention of my prime minister. He got to the boy just in time."

Richard Rodgers maintained that Brynner knew what to do at exactly the precise moment. "Not only as a performer, but of the diverse contributions he made. We'd have been in serious trouble if it hadn't been for him. Everybody came to Yul for help. Actors, young and old, sought his advice. His dressing room was complete bedlam. It was filled with policemen trying to avoid the rain, delivery and messenger boys marching in and out. A record player blared out music by Bach and Stravinsky, and Dixieland jazz. I used to wonder how he could stand such turmoil. I soon discovered that he thrived on it."

Brynner would sit serenely in the middle of all this activity. He'd squat crosslegged in his chair—when he used one. Between brief replies, he would play Monopoly or Scrabble, carefully examine some postage stamps, and reflect on his performance.

"It took me about two months to feel comfortable in the role of the king," he said. Scrub as he would, Yul could not shed the role when he went home at night. Virginia and his friends remembered how the king's personality gradually overtook him. Although he kept denying it, his habitual expression, usually one of cheerful expectancy, was replaced by one of impassive hauteur. He took to gesturing with his eyebrows. His stride lengthened. He carried his chin a little higher. His nostrils flared when he was provoked. There was a new firmness in his manner. It seemed that Yul, who had formerly equivocated about his cultural origin, had discovered an identity. He became more imperious but developed into a kindly arbitrator.

"When he thought you were in the right he'd stand up for you no matter what," said Barbara Luna, one of the royal dancers. "One time some of the other girls, myself included, were bawled out for being out of step. We complained that the music was being played much too fast. It was denied. That was when Yul came to our defense. I can still remember him saying, 'They're absolutely right! The music is too fast!' All the dancers were so pleased that we kissed him."

Another Brynner champion was Doris Dawson, an usher at the St. James Theater. "Most of the other actors took us for granted," she said. "But not him. He thanked me quite extravagantly for showing people to their seats. 'If not for you,' he told me, 'there wouldn't be any show—just chaos.' Somehow, he had found out that I was hoping to land an acting part on Broadway. During the year I worked as an usher at the St. James Theater he gave me lots of pointers. He also tipped me off in advance about auditions. On my birthday he gave me a copy of a book Michael Chekhov had written on the technique of acting."

The book, published by Harper and Row, was called *To the Actor*. Brynner was pleased when he was asked to contribute an introduction. "I know what I'm about to write is very sentimental," he said, "but it's the unvarnished truth!"

Yul's affectionate preface included a deep appreciation of his former teacher: "I came to America with the sole purpose of working with you . . . Now, holding your manuscript in my hands I have achieved my complete goal . . . [the book] is worth more than its weight in gold to every actor. In fact, I believe to every creative artist."

Yul was kind to most aspiring actors, but he had a strong aversion to understudies. "They're always waiting around for you to die," he said. He rarely allowed one to substitute for him. However, when his sister Vera starred at the New York City Opera, he took the night off to hear her sing the leading role in Gian Carlo Menotti's *The Counsel*. He was immediately recognized and besieged for autographs. He refused to give any. "This night belongs to her." Chivalrously, he said, "She is the talented member of the family."

The following day his understudy was once again idle as Yul resumed being the king. For his performance, he won every major award given to a stage actor. Among them were the Donaldson, the Antoinette Perry, the Critics' Circle.

The day after the winner of the Critics' Circle award was announced, the great-grandson of King Mongkut came to see the play. He said that he hoped his great-grandfather had been as regal as Yul. When the prince's statement was relayed to Brynner, he accepted the accolade as his due. He had been the first actor in more than a decade to win eleven out of twelve votes for the Critics' Circle award. "If he had only made that remark earlier," Brynner said. "I'm certain the judges would have been unanimous!"

Queen Juliana of the Netherlands was another member of royalty who lauded Brynner. After the performance she attended, he invited her to his apartment on Central Park

West. While the Queen's bodyguards patrolled the building, he and Virginia entertained her. She asked them for Yul's recipe for beef stroganoff and admired a rosewood coffee table he had built. When it came time for her to leave, Yul wrapped up a doggie bag of leftover beef stroganoff.

Immediately after every Saturday night performance, the three Brynners would leave Manhattan for the house they had rented in Norwalk, Connecticut, close to the Long Island Sound. Yul had bought a luxurious powerboat. Sunday mornings, he, Virginia, and young Rocky could be found trying it out and practicing their waterskiing.

For the first time in his life Brynner had money in the bank and an excellent credit rating. *Ladies' Home Journal* called him "Broadway's ideal husband." A radio show talk host invited him to give his views on matrimony. When the moderator questioned King Mongkut's marital behavior, Yul rose to the monarch's defense. "His style isn't my style," he said heatedly. "Still, I wouldn't call him an immoral man. Quite the contrary. In his own way he was more loyal and devoted to his wives than many men who go to church regularly and regard themselves as being ultrapious!"

He claimed that faithfulness was a state of being, not a legal definition. "I feel strongly," he said, "that how a man treats marriage should be strictly his own business." Yul was then asked if he felt that a man should tell his wife about an outside affair. "That depends very much on the sort of wife he had," Brynner answered. "With some wives you can be quite candid. Fortunately, I have one of those. Virginia understands me perfectly."

He didn't explain what the "perfectly" meant. In the early days of their marriage, Yul prided himself on being a faithful husband. Occasionally, however, he found it difficult to resist admiring ladies telling him how thrilling he was. But the next day he'd confess and promise Virginia that he'd never succumb again. She'd forgive him.

Soon after Yul's triumph in *The King and I*, Virginia retired from acting to devote herself full-time to her family. "In show business," she said, "catapulting from obscurity to stardom is a dizzy matter. One day you are an impoverished housewife going about your business, the next you are basking in the reflected glory of your husband's sudden fame. Your name works magic. However, some things you can never quite reconcile to have happened. You have lost your privacy. Although you can now get the best table at a restaurant, you eat your meal under the curious stares of other diners."

Unlike his wife, Yul enjoyed the attention he now received. He pretended he loathed all the fuss that was made over him, but it was very apparent that he relished it. Gertrude Lawrence said, "Yul has started collecting celebrities the way other people collect stamps. He is on a first-name basis with hundreds of VIP's. The other night he told me that *Eleanor* came backstage to tell him how much she liked him. He said that he and the former First Lady discussed children."

Undoubtedly, it was true. Mrs. Roosevelt often repeated an anecdote he had told her about his son, Rocky. The youngster's teacher asked her class what their fathers did for a living. All the other students gave routine answers: "Doctor, lawyer, businessman." When Rocky's turn came he said, "My father is a king."

Despite Brynner's newfound fame, he spent a great deal of time with his young son. Yul taught the boy how to play the guitar, how to waterski, and how to cook. Regularly, the actor would bring in cookies the youngster had made to distribute among members of the cast. While the actors were forced to eat the leatherlike cookies, Rocky's puffed-up father would say solemnly, "Imagine, and he's only a very young child!"

Marlene Dietrich was a frequent backstage visitor to the

St. James Theater. Gossip columnists reported that she and Yul were romantically involved. On his birthday she brought him a small chocolate cake. A newspaper photographer attempted to snap a picture of it. Brynner stopped him, saying, "I don't want your readers getting the wrong idea. Marlene has a much higher regard for me than just a tiny cake. But it was all she could find."

During the second year of the show, Gertrude Lawrence came down with cancer. She claimed it was hepatitis. Her singing and dancing fell off, but she insisted on continuing with the role of Mrs. Anna. When an understudy was asked to take over, she became very angry and appealed to Yul for help. Although he tried to shield her, the audience felt they were being cheated when she appeared. Admirers who had formerly cheered Gertrude started ridiculing her. Several times, Brynner had to be restrained from leaping off the stage to silence the offenders.

Gertrude Lawrence died on September 7, 1952. She was buried in one of the gowns she had worn in the show. When Oscar Hammerstein informed Yul that he would now get top billing, Brynner started to cry. "He told me—and I believed him," said Hammerstein, "that losing Gertie was a tremendous price to pay for advancement. It was the only time I ever saw him cry."

"When she died," Brynner said, "some of me died, too. The part of Anna was played by other fine actresses. There were Celeste Holm, Constance Towers, Constance Carpenter, Anna Mary Dickey, Patricia Morrison, Virginia McKenna, Mary Beth Piel, and others. They were good. But for me there always will be one Anna—Gertrude Lawrence. I was miserable without her. I missed her terribly, her corny jokes. She was the one who said I was the only person in the world to have five-o'clock shadow on his head."

For several weeks following Gertrude's death, Yul shunned his dressing room. He would arrive at the theater

just in time to apply his makeup. Promptly after it was removed he would leave for home. His only relaxation seemed
to be attending baseball games. He had always been an enthusiastic fan. Once during the World Series he devised a
plan whereby the orchestra leader flashed him signs about
the progress of the game while he was on stage for a matinee.
Now, he sat moodily in his reserved box seat. His melancholy
was broken when he caught a pop foul that had grazed his
bare head. He laughed as he said, "Gertie would tell me that
my head finally had some use."

After *The King and I* closed its Broadway run, it went on
tour. The first stop was Hershey, Pennsylvania, the home of
the famous candy bar. The Brynners arrived late at night,
but Yul insisted on showing Rocky the intersection of Chocolate Street and Vanilla Avenue. The mayor was alerted. The
following morning he gave Yul a carton filled with Hershey
bars. "They were supposed to last for the entire tour," Virginia said. "But my husband and Rocky finished them in
one day. It was hard to know who was the bigger child."

In Salt Lake City, the youngsters in the cast—Chinese,
Korean, Japanese, Puerto Rican—were taken by Brynner on
a picnic. He had selected an amusement park that had rides
and a swimming pool. But when they tried to enter they
were barred. "Some of those kids are colored!" a guard told
them. "You can't go in!"

Yul was furious and started shouting. The manager,
who had heard all the commotion, came running out. He
recognized Brynner. "I'll make an exception in your case,"
he said apologetically. "You and the children are most welcome."

Yul refused the special privilege. "Take your park and
you know what you can do with it?" he snapped. When a
reporter wrote a story about the incident, Brynner was invited to address students in several segregated schools.

In one Los Angeles school, his audience consisted mainly

of boys and girls from minority families. They cheered when he told them, "You constantly hear that every youngster in the United States can grow up to become president. But you and I know that's a lot of claptrap. Perhaps in the future. Certainly not now if you're not from the right group. However, your chances to succeed are greatly increased by the amount of education you have. I strongly urge you to stay in school. Of course, your chances will increase tremendously if you're as talented as Marian Anderson, Jackie Robinson, or Yul Brynner."

When the company came to Chicago, Yul was invited to address a group of student-actors at Northwestern University. Although he had oriented his lecture around the theater, it was attended by dozens of spectators far removed from the drama department. One history professor labeled the speech "Brynner's Memorable Message to Would-be Actors and Etceteras." It offered a splendid opportunity to decipher some of Yul's unconventional views. Here are several excerpts:

> *Doomsayers tell you that no matter how good you are, your chances of achieving recognition are practically nonexistent. And that even if you are the one in ten thousand that beats the odds, you will be facing a flock of difficult and disappointing years. Well, these perpetual Cassandras may be right—up to a point . . .*
>
> *Yes, the going will be tough—especially if you're a weakling. However, if it isn't, I suggest you start worrying. Yes, there will be difficult and disappointing years—especially if you're a weakling. But I'll wager that you won't want to ever forget them. Meanwhile, I give you the Brynner Plan for making your path to success a little less painful . . .*
>
> *First off, begin with creating individuality. What do I mean by that? If you ask five artists to paint the same scene, I feel*

certain that all five paintings won't be exactly alike. They are not cameras. Neither should you be. The chief curse of modern mankind is uniformity. That's so wrong.

Each one of us should be known for possessing something unique. If you're not going to be jailed because of that peculiarity, I recommend that you go public with it. So what if you're called whimsical, dreamer, oddball, or even kooky? At least you will be called . . .

Give more consideration to your body. Make it your best line of defense as well as offense. Train it to express joy, sorrow, pity, anxiety, honesty, sorrow, etcetera. This can be done by enlarging the circle of your interests. Study those you believe excel in these areas. Concentrate on the leaders. Study their reactions, their points of view, their concepts, their opinions. Try to find out why they feel this way.

But don't allow them to overawe you! Under no circumstances should you grant them that privilege. I've found that the moment you allow someone to feel he's superior, you are in for serious heartaches. After all, Hamlet was just another guy . . .

The next step is to develop your imagination. As of now it is probably limited to your past and present—things you did or are doing. Undoubtedly, you have daydreams. But if you're like most people, you decide that they are just that—daydreams. Well, start pretending. Start thinking about the future. Start exerting your ego.

I'm not suggesting that you begin living a life of complete make-believe, but why not try just a little of it? Look more intently into your own image. Remember that success isn't immoral.

Soon after Yul's academic performance, he announced that he would leave the show. Because of his departure, advance ticket sales slumped sharply. The producers decided that it was foolish to continue the tour without him. "There is only one King," the Chicago *Tribune* had written. When the final curtain came down, Brynner, accompanied by his wife and son, were rushed to the airport in a siren-shrieking police car. The following morning in Hollywood, the King of Siam became the Pharaoh of Egypt.

- CHAPTER FIVE -

H.R.H.
Goes to
Hollywood

DURING Brynner's appearance in *The King and I* he permitted no outsider backstage between acts. "I was so busy creating the proper image that I wasn't going to allow anyone to jeopardize it," he said. "Or so I thought. One night late in fifty-three or it may have been early in fifty-four, right after the first act ended, I was told that Cecil B. DeMille wanted to see me. I was about to repeat my no-visitor rule when it hit me that one of the all-time greats in the movie industry was calling. Why, he was a legend—he had made Hollywood's first feature film, *The Squaw Man*. I had always marveled at his genius. Instead of being annoyed, I said, 'Show Mr. DeMille in.'

"A few seconds later a distinguished-looking man of about seventy-five came into my dressing room. I shall always remember his first words: 'How would you like to appear in a motion picture that your grandchildren and great-grandchildren will rave about?' Of course I was interested. I don't think anyone in his right mind wouldn't be."

DeMille also recalled that meeting. In his autobiography he wrote: "At the end of the first act, I went backstage and found the dressing room of Yul Brynner, whom I had never met. I told him that I was planning to make a movie called

The Ten Commandments. There aren't many minutes between the acts of a Broadway musical, but in that space of time I told him the story of Pharaoh Rameses II. I offered him the part. He accepted. We shook hands. I went back to my seat. Brynner went back to being the King of Siam."

The next morning at breakfast Yul told his wife about DeMille's proposal. "Never before had I seen her so excited," he said. "Although she had received excellent notices in *Dear Ruth*, it was quite apparent that she still preferred to live near Hollywood. We had just bought a house in Connecticut, but she was ready to pack and return to the West Coast. I had to caution her that it wasn't going to happen for at least a year. Probably a lot longer, from the way the public was flocking to *The King and I.*"

DeMille wasn't the only one interested in Brynner. Shortly after the show opened on Broadway, film director Billy Wilder wanted him to star in a movie called *A New Kind of Love*. Yul was paid $15,000 upon his acceptance. But due to a series of casting complications the movie was called off. Audrey Hepburn had originally been chosen to be the leading lady. She backed out because of a prior engagement that lasted longer than she had anticipated. Then Wilder announced that Katharine Hepburn would take over. She, too, had to withdraw. Casting difficulties had plagued the film from the start. Maurice Chevalier had been scheduled to play the male lead, but the State Department had refused to issue him a visa because he had signed the antiwar Stockholm Peace Appeal.

When the decision was finally made to scrap the projected movie, Brynner appeared relieved. "It's just as well," he said. "In my time I've signed lots of things. Who knows what the State Department will object to next. Besides, I had given my word to DeMille."

The Ten Commandments was a new version of a silent movie DeMille had made in 1927. At the time it had been considered one of Hollywood's unmatchable films. However, the new edition was far more grandiose. It cost $13 million and employed 25,000 extras. For three hours and thirty-nine minutes it told the Old Testament story of how the Jews were held in bondage until Moses [Charlton Heston], who had fled because he had killed an Egyptian, delivered them from Pharaoh's tyranny.

"I guess the reason why I felt so close to Mr. DeMille was that he thought like me," Brynner said. "On a grand scale."

Under DeMille's tutelage, he became an extension of the older man's mind and behavior. Although they often worked together in almost complete silence, they seemed to share similar objectives. Yul explained it as being "a kind of pantomime." If DeMille liked something he did, he would nod and wave his pinky finger. If he didn't approve, he'd shrug and pinch his nose.

Sam Cavanaugh, a cameraman assigned to the film, had worked on some of DeMille's previous movies. "I knew from experience," he said, "that he wouldn't tolerate the slightest interference. Why, he'd stamp off the set if anyone dared to raise their voice. But it was very different in the case of Brynner. It was as if DeMille was paying very close attention to a very intelligent, favorite child."

During a scene where Pharaoh had to give Moses some orders, Yul felt that it would be more effective if he relayed his displeasure to one of his subordinates. "A man in power always delegates orders," he told DeMille.

"The old man took the advice without a murmur," said Cavanaugh. "Later the script called for a mob to try and tell Pharaoh its troubles—almost one at a time. Yul thought it would be more striking if they all babbled simultaneously. DeMille agreed and reshaped the entire scene."

While Brynner was playing the terrible-tempered Pharaoh, Edward G. Robinson, who had been cast as the evil Dathan, presented him with a rabbit's foot "to help you catch Moses before he makes his getaway in the Red Sea."

"Thank God, Moses wasn't halted," Yul said. "But that rabbit's foot sure helped me enjoy one of the luckiest days of my life. In a twenty-four-hour period, I won at poker, the studio baseball pool, a radio quiz show, and walked away from a serious car crash. Try and top that!"

He boasted so much that the usually uninfluenced DeMille asked him to wave the rabbit's foot around the lot where a section of the movie was being filmed. Yul said that he would have liked to but he had given the rabbit's foot to his young son who had promptly lost it. Despite the good-luck charm's absence, *The Ten Commandments* turned out to be one of Hollywood's all-time blockbusters. The critics called it a classic.

Even though the movie had received glowing reviews, Yul didn't think too much of it. "I rarely watch a film I'm in," he said. "But I saw that one when it premiered. I didn't enjoy that performance I gave. There were dozens of things I could have improved upon. You must realize that by the time the movie is shown to the public it's often well over a year after it was actually made. In that time the actor—if he's any good—has learned new approaches, has new standards. He wishes he could do it over again.

"Charlie Chaplin was like that. He felt that half of Hollywood releases should have been stored in mothballs for at least a year. After that they should be reexamined and reshot. He said the reason it wasn't done was because of greedy studio executives. Charlie also attacked actors who demanded early releases. 'The only reason they do it is to prove they're still in demand. 'Let's face it, Yul,' he said. 'So many people in our business are insecure.' "

The Brynners rarely entertained anyone connected with films. They preferred the company of professors from the University of California, where Virginia had been a student.

Their selectivity caused columnist Hedda Hopper to ask: "What totally bald actor regards himself as being too good for his peers?"

When the Brynners first arrived on the West Coast they lived in hotel rooms or furnished apartments. Eventually, they bought a small white clapboard house in West Los Angeles.

"By Hollywood standards it was very unpretentious," Virginia said. "It didn't have a swimming pool or even a built-in barbecue pit. Yul had wanted something more elegant, but I held out for simplicity. That was one of the few times I won out."

Reporters were discouraged from seeing the inside. "My personal life belongs solely to me," Brynner said. Edward R. Murrow invited him to be interviewed for the *Person to Person* TV program. Yul agreed only on the condition that it take place in his dressing room or in a hotel. It's too bad it never happened—a discussion between these two gifted conversationalists would have been stimulating.

Virginia, who had studied journalism in college, was friendly with many writers. She invited one to tour the house. The resulting story revealed that the Brynner living room was dominated by a large, red velvet throne. Above it was a framed picture of Yul and the inscription: *Long Live the King*. While the magazine was on the newsstands Yul refused to talk to his wife. He spent his free time playing word games with seven-year-old Rocky or tinkering with his custom-made Mercedes roadster.

One Sunday afternoon during this period a visiting professor from Cambridge University came to the house. He complained that his American-built car was only getting ten miles to the gallon. Yul, who regarded himself as an expert mechanic, assured him that he could quickly remedy the trouble. Majestically, he lifted the hood, looked inside, and started pulling out the moving parts. Each time he pried one loose he rewarded himself with a vodka martini. When the automobile was almost stripped bare, a very drunken Brynner said to his equally drunken guest, "Perhaps we should call another mechanic?"

Virginia, who had observed the bibulous scene from the kitchen window, decided that the time had come for a peace offering. She prepared a fresh pitcher of martinis and took them out to the lawn. When Yul saw what she had done he announced that all was forgiven. Soon, an intoxicated husband, wife, and English professor were quoting Shakespeare, reciting Irish limericks, and singing Victorian ballads. They made such a racket that the police were called.

"It was not an uncommon sight," said a neighbor. "That place seemed to be fueled by whiskey."

If Yul and Virginia drank together and preferred entertaining only highbrows, they also quarreled frequently. She recalled one of their most furious fights. "For the life of me I don't remember what set it off," she said. "But for more than an hour we called each other the vilest names. We screamed. We scratched. We wrestled. It ended when I tripped over a chair. The next thing I knew we were in each other's arms kissing."

Despite Yul's strong affection for alcohol, he rarely missed a scheduled shooting. Bleary-eyed, he'd arrive on the set before 6 A.M. and invariably quote an old gypsy proverb: "A pity to the man who allows wine to sadden his day."

Most reviewers were enthusiastic about the way he had played Pharaoh. A few felt that he was still being the King of Siam. "He makes a superb ruler of Egypt," one critic wrote. "And why not? With a plentitude of training in *The King and I*, he knows a good thing when he sees it. His Royal Highness has simply shifted locations from the Far East to the Near East."

DeMille rejected that analysis. "I advise this so-called expert to compare Yul's performance in *The King and I* and

The Ten Commandments in quick succession," he said. "He will quickly notice numerous subtle differences in characterization between the barbaric, puzzled, arrogantly defensive King of Siam and the ruthless, arrogant, but sophisticated, self-assured Pharaoh. Yes, a few similarities exist. However, it's the subtle differences which demonstrate his great artistic competence."

Yul was a favorite whipping boy of Hedda Hopper, who was well known for her acrimonious screen reporting. Her wrath was undoubtedly the result of his having once called her writing "a pack of fantasies tied not so neatly in violet toilet paper."

She described his Pharaoh role as "a gypsy swindle . . . Brynner the King is never dead; he just dusts off his crown and plays him over again." A previous Hopper column said that he rode around the studio lot on a red and white bicycle that had a large sign attached to it:

> *My name is Brynner*
> *And it rhymes with sinner.*

Yul replied promptly:

> *Hedda's bike story is so much pap,*
> *And believe me it rhymes with crap.*

She also accused him of pretending to be an international gourmet. "Yul Brynner's knowledge of food comes from his eating like a pig," she told her readers. "The truth is that he'll devour anything, even dog chow. What's more, he'll claim it's heavenly."

There was some truth to Hopper's statement. Hank Mitchell, who used to handle publicity for Paramount, spoke of Yul's eating habits. "He'd arrive on the set famished," he recalled. "Immediately, he'd start eating. It never stopped.

In between regular meals he'd demand the strangest snacks—fried cactus spines and rattlesnake tidbits."

Anne Baxter was Nefertiti in *The Ten Commandments.* "While we were making the movie I often had lunch with him," she said. "Once I told him that if I ate the way he did I'd soon be hired as the fat lady in the circus. He just nodded and said seriously that it was all a matter of proper exercise. Then right in the middle of the dining room he pushed back his chair and started doing pushups."

DeMille wanted to star Brynner in another of his movies. "Yul is the most powerful personality I've ever seen on the screen," the veteran director and producer said. "A cross between Douglas Fairbanks, Sr., Apollo, and a little bit of Hercules."

Yul thanked him for the lavish compliment but refused his request. "I'm on leave of absence," he explained, and returned to CBS. He wasn't allowed much time to devote to television, however. Several weeks later he was approached by 20th Century-Fox to appear in the film version of *The King and I.*

"I knew they were going to ask me," Brynner said. "Still I was pleased when the offer was made. However, months before I had decided that this time I would do the directing and get someone else for the part of the king. I wanted Marlon Brando. We talked about it, but he turned the role down. It's too bad, because I've always felt that he would have made a fascinating King Mongkut."

Charles Brackett, the movie's producer, urged Yul to reconsider. He offered him $300,000 plus a percentage of the profits. "After a great deal of soul-searching I agreed to once again play the king," Yul said. "Believe me when I tell you that money wasn't the deciding factor. The truth is that I realized that I hadn't even scratched the surface of the king's contradictory complexities. You have to know him a long time to really understand him. I suppose the reason I finally said yes was because I'd grown fond of him and hated the thought of bidding him farewell. I decided it would be a challenge to play him on the screen."

Harvey Grant, a studio executive, did some of the negotiating. "My hair or what's left of it started falling out after our first meeting," he said. "I'm certain Brynner wanted to sign, but out of sheer orneriness he made things difficult. He put up every obstacle you can think of. First he wanted script approval. When that was allowed he insisted on cast approval. Every day there'd be something else. Once we were very close to calling it all off—and for the oddest reason. I had noticed a newspaper article that listed his height as a 'shade under six feet.' Innocently, I said that it must have been an error because I was six feet and was about three inches taller than he. You'd think I had said that his mother was a whore from the way he reacted."

Throughout his life Yul was sensitive about how tall the public thought he was. He refused to divulge exact measurements. When a 20th Century-Fox release said he was five feet, nine inches, he charged into Grant's office and called him a scheming perjurer."

To help publicize the forthcoming film, the studio gave a gala black-tie party. There, Brynner was friendly until he discovered he was talking to a 20th Century-Fox executive. "The moment he did," recalled one of the guests, "his lynching spirit came out. When I told him I was a vice president he started calling me every name in the book. In his opinion all studio officials were brainless asses. He kept babbling how we prevented him from playing Richard III, Ahab, King Lear, and Shaw's Caesar."

Three decades later, people who were there still speak of that party. "Yul's biochemistry made him supercharged," recalled Helen Boyd, a secretary who had been responsible for the seating arrangements. "He spent the first half of the party in the kitchen entertaining the cooks and waiters with some of his gypsy songs. But when he was asked to mingle with the partygoers, he was utterly unsociable."

During the shooting of *The King and I* Yul became very irritated with the producer of the film. "He would try to goad me," Brackett recalled. "Threaten to walk off the set if his ideas weren't instantly adopted. In story conferences he'd always have the last word. The moment he'd squat on the floor like a baseball catcher I could be certain that I was in for a lecture."

Brynner explained the reason for the strange position. He said that it had been taught to him by his gypsy grand-mother. "There's an excellent reason for sitting that way," he'd say. "It's sure to wear your opponent down. He's so busy looking at you that he's bound to forget what he was going to say."

Sometimes, Yul would offer another version: "I picked up the habit when I lived in Peking. At the end of the day the Chinese farmers would sit like that in the dusk of the evening. They'd sit for hours, smoking those long-stemmed pipes and surveying their rice fields. Not a move. Just sit there and think."

Another person Yul constantly fought with was Walter Lang, the director. Brynner would tell Lang that everything he did was wrong. "If you didn't agree with him," the di-rector said, "you could expect to be called a bloody fool or lots worse. He would claim that he was really the picture's director, that I wasn't needed. That without him calling the shots the movie would wind up being second rate."

Deborah Kerr, the film's Mrs. Anna, usually very de-mure, became almost rapturous when she discussed Bryn-ner. "His imaginative suggestions and instructions were responsible for turning *The King and I* into a great movie. If not for him it would have wound up being just another pleasant Hollywood musical. He had a wonderful way of handling actors—got things out of them they never realized they possessed. Nothing escaped him—he was interested in the most minor scene. I will always be grateful for his making me look far better than I really am."

When Yul received an Oscar nomination for his acting and Lang received one for directing, Kerr sent Brynner a congratulatory wire: "A WELL DESERVED DOUBLE VICTORY. NOT ONLY ARE YOU A MARVELOUS ACTOR BUT A MARVELOUS DIRECTOR."

Yul saw to it that all the ingredients that made the stage production memorable were faithfully transferred to the screen. In addition, he added dozens of subtle expressions and movements. Because of him the movie suggested a stronger feeling between Anna and the King. It was done with nothing more than the meeting of eyes and the caress of a hand in his deathbed scene.

Although *The King and I* was made after *The Ten Commandments*, 20th Century-Fox released it four months earlier. The reviews were ecstatic. *Variety*: "The larger exposure via the film medium should make Brynner an international personality. The movie is the bombshell of the year . . . Yul's incisive use of body, voice, and gestures plus his physical appearance give authority to his kingly role. His completely shaven head should do for baldheaded men what Pinza did for the middle aged." *New York Herald Tribune*: "It is Brynner who gives the film its animal spark. He is every inch an oriental King, from eloquent fingers that punctuate his commands to the sinewy, barefooted legs. He stalks about the palace like an impatient leopard. His eyes glower with imperial rage, they widen with boyish curiosity, they dance at his own simple jokes, and on his death couch, they are heavy with resignation and accumulated wisdom. This is a rare bit of acting—Brynner is the King!"

The thirty-three-year-old widow of a millionaire Texas oilman was so stirred by his portrayal of the king that she instructed her lawyers to take out ads in several leading newspapers. However, her copy was so lurid it was turned down. Arthur Godfrey, a well-known TV variety show host, spent a large portion of his program discussing the incident. He invited Brynner to be his guest, but Ted Ashley, who was then Yul's agent, advised against it.

Yul was rapidly emerging as a new screen phenomenon. "Every studio wanted him," said Ashley. "They were willing to pay tremendous prices. Never have I known another star so sought after."

Brynner sifted through many offers. He chose to make *Anastasia* for 20th Century-Fox. "I figured that I might as well do it for them," he said resignedly. "One studio is as bad as the next. Besides, I felt that Ingrid Bergman would make a wonderful costar. I thought she had suffered enough—that it was high time to bring her back to the U.S. screen."

Seven years before, the Bergman affair had been Hollywood's most notorious scandal. The actress, who at the time was the biggest box-office attraction, had deserted her husband, Peter Lindstrom, and her eleven-year-old daughter, Pia, to run off with Italian movie director Roberto Rossellini. She had borne him a child out of wedlock. The press labeled Ingrid's behavior reprehensible, which resulted in her being blackballed by American movie makers.

Yul was incensed at her banishment and vowed to bring her back. "This was my golden opportunity," he said. "So what if Ingrid had not behaved properly? It was her affair, and hers alone. Too many people believe that the price of an admission ticket enables them to peek through windows. That thought is pure rubbish. The public is entitled to a fine performance—and that's all!"

In the movie, Yul was cast as the deceitful General Bounine, a former White Russian army officer. He wants to palm off Anna Anderson (Ingrid Bergman), haggard and starving Russian castaway, as the daughter of Czar Nicholas II. On the morning of July 17, 1918, the Czar and his entire family were murdered. Stories began circulating that the sixteen-year-old Anastasia had miraculously escaped. Bounine wants to get his hands on the £10 million the late Russian ruler had deposited in the Bank of England.

Relentlessly, he coaches his protegée about Anastasia's childhood. He is startled when she appears to possess an intimate knowledge of the royal family. She is gradually transformed into a beautiful, self-confident woman. Bounine ends up not only falling in love with her, but believing she is the real Anastasia.

During the filming, Ingrid's daily mail was filled with vituperative letters. They affected her acting. "She'd forget her lines, bump into chairs, and face the wrong camera," Yul said. "I tried to calm her down."

One spring evening he invited her to accompany him to a roller-skating rink. As soon as they laced on their skates she kept slipping, and he kept propping her up. They were in the midst of this routine when a very irate woman who identified herself as being a visiting housewife from Pittsburgh glided over. "You're nothing but a slut and a hussy!" she yelled at Bergman. Then she turned to Yul, who looked as if he was about to strike her, and said, "You should have had more sense than to make a movie with her."

Instead of replying, Yul reached for Ingrid's hand and together they turned their backs and made their way to a nearby bench. But a few minutes later he resumed skating by himself and deliberately plowed into the woman who had insulted Ingrid. As she lay sprawled on the ground he said sweetly, "Madam, I do hope the bruises on your ass heal slowly!"

In early July 1956, while the movie was still in production, Ed Sullivan, MC of a popular Sunday night television program, asked his viewers to tell him if Ingrid Bergman should be allowed to visit the United States. "Write, wire, or phone," he pleaded.

Brynner immediately sent Sullivan a cablegram: "IT'S NONE OF YOUR RUDDY BUSINESS WHAT SHE DOES BUT IF YOU MUST KNOW THE ANSWER IS YES YES YES!"

"Ingrid needn't have worried," said Anatole Litvak, the film's director. "*Anastasia* won for her an Oscar. Yul was the big reason. Somehow he could always make her smile. He, too, deserved an Academy Award for his performance of Bounine. But I'm sure the reason he didn't get one was because of his sensational performance in *The King and I.*"

For his acting in that movie Yul was named the best male lead of 1956 by the National Board of Review of Motion Pictures. He had stiff competition: Sir Laurence Olivier in *Richard III*, Kirk Douglas in *Lust for Life*, James Dean and Rock Hudson in *Giant*. At a party Yul attended after the ceremony, he was called upon to make a speech. Brynner, who had been drinking heavily, quoted his friend Jean Cocteau, the French playwright and novelist.

"Jean gave me some excellent advice I want to share with all of you," he said. "Jean told me that when you see yourself becoming famous, you should never let anybody think you go to the bathroom." A very embarrassed Virginia tried to quiet her husband, but he shook her away. Swaying badly, he continued speaking: "You must never allow your fans to connect you with excretion."

The next day Hudson sent him a couplet he had written:

No matter what you were told by Jean Cocteau
When you got to go, you got to go.

Yul, who had always loved rhymes, wrote one of his own:

I recommend Cocteau's good advice
Winning an Oscar is very, very nice.

It's rare for an actor to have more than one hit picture released in a single year. Brynner had three: *The King and I*, *The Ten Commandments*, and *Anastasia*. At the time a favorite Hollywood parlor game was to try and guess why he had suddenly become so prominent. Four actresses whose names had been romantically linked with his provided some answers. To Ingrid Bergman, he was "like Abraham Lincoln—he helped free me." Anne Baxter called him "an egghead Clark Gable," and Joan Crawford said "He's the new Rudolph Valentino." But Deborah Kerr said, "He doesn't resemble anyone else. Yul is strictly Yul. He isn't particularly tall, has strong Mongol features, and is bald. But on him it all looks good. He is very, very handsome and very, very sensual."

That year Brynner earned more than $750,000. "It was such easy money," he told his friend Sidney Lumet, "that I've decided to remain in Hollywood."

"But Hollywood is so full of crap," Lumet said.

"Sidney, they don't yet know what crap is!" Yul replied.

CHAPTER SIX

Mangled
By the
Movies

ALTHOUGH Brynner became a box-office phenomenon, he felt that he had been savaged by motion pictures. Each time he finished a movie he'd complain to Virginia that there was a major difference in outlook between Broadway and Hollywood. "The theater respects talent and straightforwardly moans or cheers it," he told her. "Hollywood flatters you no matter what—their sole evaluation is profit!"

According to him, many of the biggest film stars couldn't act "a bagel's hole worth." He said that several of them had confided in him that they were afraid to appear on Broadway because they realized they couldn't fool a sophisticated stage audience. "Their lack of ability on the movie lots is catching," he'd say sadly. "Suddenly you find yourself settling for a lesser performance."

Many people are unaware of how many shoddy pictures Brynner made and how badly they were received by the critics. A thinner-skinned man might have been considerably upset, not to say discouraged, as one movie after another was ridiculed. His diminished status didn't come all at once—it occurred slowly. Following *Anastasia* he was seen as the violent, dissolute Dmitri in a film version of Fyodor Dostoyevsky's novel *The Brothers Karamazov* (1958). Yul was cast as a Russian army officer who was notorious for his gambling and wenching. Dmitri is badly in debt and in constant conflict with his father (Lee J. Cobb). Both of them lust for Grushenka (Maria Schell), an angelic-looking coquette. Dmitri publicly threatens to kill his father. When his father is murdered, it is assumed that he is the culprit. But he manages to escape, taking Grushenka with him.

Considering the large problem of condensing Dostoyevsky's involved classic of hate, greed, vengeance, and salvation into two and a half hours, Brynner warily expected some adverse response. He was astonished when the United States government selected *The Brothers Karamazov* for its official entry to the Cannes Film Festival. Yul agreed to Washington's request that he personally represent the movie. An Air Force plane flew him to Nice.

The audience of 1200 wildly applauded him when he appeared on the stage before the showing. However, loud catcalls and razzing drowned out the few polite handclaps when the movie ended. As Yul rose to take a final bow, viewers stood on their seats and shook their fists.

Most critics shared their opinion. One Paris reviewer said, "Not the greatest failure but very near it . . . Perhaps it isn't Brynner's fault? The director and producer should share the blame. Whenever Brynner appeared ready to burst out, it seemed that someone was holding him back."

Pandro Berman, the producer of *The Brothers Karamazov*, angrily disagreed. "If ever an actor was given leeway it was Yul," he said. "He demanded it—and got it. I've always believed that he did a fine job in that picture. But some people weren't satisfied with just a fine job. They were determined to be treated to a super-excellent performance. Anything less was not acceptable."

In addition to his acting, Berman was impressed by Brynner's constant exuberance. "The movie called for some wild gypsy music," he recalled. "As soon as the balalaika sounded, he'd begin to whirl around. I once asked him where he got so much energy. He said it was left over from the time he'd worked in the circus. Then he patted his stomach. 'You can drive a truck over my belly,' he bragged."

Throughout his life Brynner prided himself on his strength and vitality. On the coldest days during the filming of *The Brothers Karamazov* he'd strut around the set barechested. Other male actors in the cast tried to copy him. "They gave up when they began to shiver and sneeze," Brynner said. "I like most Americans, but they've been ruined by central heating and cashmere sweaters. Stuntmen are called in for the most trivial undertakings."

His insistence on not allowing anyone to stand in for him almost caused a serious delay in completing the movie. One scene called for him to do some trick riding. He mounted the horse gracefully and brought him to a full gallop. Suddenly, the horse stumbled and Yul was tossed off. It was very obvious that Brynner was hurt, but he demanded to be allowed to finish the scene. The following day when he had trouble breathing a doctor was called. X-rays revealed four broken rib bones. He was warned to rest for several weeks.

"That doctor figured wrong," Yul said. "I saw him on Friday. On the following Monday I was back before the camera. I suppose if I had been some pantywaisted Hollywood actor I would have stayed out for six months. Why, the ones who regard themselves as two-fisted he-men take days off for a hangnail!"

Once, talking to DeMille, he defended his stuntman position. "A great deal of characterization goes into the way you walk, run, stumble, sit a horse," he said. "If you constantly allow someone else to pretend they're you, you're cheating the viewer—and yourself."

DeMille, who was known for realism in his films, agreed

but felt there were times when stuntmen were necessary. "Some actors are much too valuable to be allowed to be injured," he said.

"What if the stuntman is hurt?" Brynner snapped. "Doesn't he count?"

"It's his job," DeMille replied. "Besides, he's more expendable."

"That's very callous!" Yul said.

It was a real quarrel and not a very good beginning for the job he had just undertaken. He had promised DeMille that he would direct a remake of *The Buccaneer*, a film DeMille had made twenty-one years before. Now, Yul had second thoughts. No one, not even DeMille, could tell him he was wrong. Brynner threatened to bow out completely, but after a great deal of persuasive arm-twisting agreed to star in the film. "But I'll do nothing else!" he said emphatically.

Anthony Quinn, then DeMille's son-in-law, became the director. Yul was cast as the swashbuckling pirate Jean Lafitte who helped General Andrew Jackson (Charlton Heston) win the War of 1812. Lafitte didn't wear the conventional black eye patch or sport a peg leg. Instead, he was somewhat of a dandy who appeared happier at a New Orleans cotillion than on a poop deck.

There was constant friction between Brynner and Quinn. It began when the director wanted the bald actor to wear an orange-colored wig. Yul rebelled. He finally settled for a much tamer color that was frequently covered by a broad straw hat. There was trouble again several days later when Yul was supposed to leap from a tall mast into the water. Quinn yelled for a stuntman. Brynner insisted in doing it by himself.

"I'm the director!" Quinn shouted.

"I said that I would do it," Yul replied. He yelled, "Camera!" and ran to the mast. He started climbing, and when he reached the top, he jumped. It was executed so well that a retake wasn't necessary. As soon as Brynner swam back to land he thumbed his nose at a very angry and chagrined Quinn.

"But to everyone else, Yul was very sweet and considerate," said Rebecca Morelli, who was a script girl on the movie. She still lives in Los Angeles, where she now owns a small florist shop. "When I opened my store he was one of my first customers. He came in and bought two dozen red roses. Then he wrote out a card: 'To Becky Morelli. Good luck. Your devoted fan, Yul.' "

The Buccaneer (1958) was panned by most critics. Probably the most devasting review appeared in *Time* magazine: "Yul Brynner wears a curly, reddish-brown confection on his head that suggests a sensitive blend of Bonaparte, Presley, and a well-kept Irish setter. The picture will surely prove for many moviegoers, no less than it was for actor Brynner, a hair-raising experience."

When he completed the movie, Virginia insisted that he take a much-needed rest. "Yul looked gaunt. His only relaxation seemed to be cigarettes—he was smoking fiercely. As soon as he finished one he'd light up another. Alarmed, I suggested hypnosis to get him off the habit. Yul agreed to give it a try. The hypnotist made him believe that all cigarettes tasted like castor oil."

That was a challenge to Brynner. He made the rounds of all tobacco shops buying pack after pack, trying to find one that tasted like tobacco. Two weeks later, the tobacco taste returned and Yul resumed smoking.

In March of 1958, Brynner traveled to Austria to costar with Deborah Kerr in an MGM movie about the aftermath of the recent Hungarian uprising. In *The Journey* (1959) he played Nikolai Surov, a strict but compassionate Russian major who defies orders to halt those fleeing the country. Surov refuses to stop refugees headed for the Austrian border. "All people should be allowed to live and love freely," he says.

Anatole Litvak, the movie's director and producer, invited the local press to meet the cast. At the outset Brynner made a favorable impression. He toasted the reporters and told them, "Down deep all of us, if given a decent chance, are humane. Journalists head the list." His behavior changed abruptly when he was asked questions about his birthplace and personal life. Always evasive about his background, he became belligerent and refused to respond. "It's none of your bloody business," he told them.

"What's the matter?" one of them asked. "Are you ashamed of your nationality?"

The next day a local Viennese columnist said that Brynner's real name was Julius Bruenner, and that he had never been closer to Mongolia than Hollywood. A picture of Yul accompanied the story. It was a shot of the back of his head and ears, which looked like a grapefruit between two lemons. The caption below it was: "Scarecrow Brynner, go home. We don't want you!"

In the next few months most of the Austrian newspapers continued to lambaste Yul. He was accused of spreading American propaganda in the guise of a motion picture. Matters were made worse when he was constantly seen in the company of a nineteen-year-old model. They had adjoining hotel rooms. Asked about it, he didn't resort to his standard reply of its being "none of your bloody business." Instead he said, "We're just good friends." Then he laughed as he added, "Isn't that what I'm supposed to say?"

Yul ceased laughing when the model charged him with fathering her unborn child. Privately he admitted that he may have been responsible, but publicly he denied it. This time the Austrian newspapers were filled with stories about the baldheaded American actor who refused to honor his obligation. Reporters kept hounding him. When he discovered one in his bedroom closet he made an out-of-court settlement with the model.

Virginia separated from her husband several times. Because of their young son, there was always a reconciliation. "Sometimes I felt like Yul's parent," she said. "He'd try and justify himself like some callow teenager who can't understand why he's being disciplined. His reasoning was juvenile, to say the least."

She recalled the first time he was involved with another woman, a red-haired divorcée he'd met at a party. When Virginia confronted him he didn't deny it—just looked incredulous that he had been called to account. "What was I expected to do?" he asked. "Ignore her? If I hadn't paid her any mind, she would have regarded herself as a total failure. After all, would you want to be married to a man that women didn't find attractive?"

One of Brynner's former girlfriends, an actress who was recently wed for the third time, admits to having had a stormy affair with him. "What he possessed could be best summed up in two words—animal magnetism," she said. "It was a strange combination of almost brute strength and a subtly gentle tenderness. He took complete command the moment he walked into a room. When he spoke he gave you the impression that he was speaking to you alone. He didn't look at you—he stared at you. When you looked into his eyes you felt that you had gone back centuries. It was as if a spell had suddenly been cast on you."

After each extramarital misadventure, Yul would become a model husband for a few weeks, showering Virginia with lavish but unconventional gifts. Once he gave her a samovar that played *Orchichanya* when the tea was poured. Virginia said that she found it difficult to be angry with him. "Basically he was a compassionate person, but very, very arrogant," she recalled. "The only other man that matched his vanity was his friend Jean Cocteau. Yul seemed to take lessons from him."

As a favor to Cocteau, Brynner did a guest bit in *Le*

Testament d'Orphée, a movie that was a tribute to the French surrealist author. It was written by Cocteau, directed by Cocteau, and had Cocteau playing Cocteau. Brynner claimed that he had helped fashion the perplexing story line: Cocteau's spiritual search for himself in a world full of phantoms and symbols.

Yul's part was that of a tuxedo-wearing gateman who guards the entrance to hell. His assistants were also clad in tuxedos and had completely bald heads. Other cast members were artist Pablo Picasso, bullfighter Luis Dominguin, writer Françoise Sagan.

"Jean was very interested in hell," Yul said. "So am I. We purposely chose Les Beaux-de-Provence for the setting of the movie because Dante had lived there when he wrote the *Inferno.* It gave you an eerie feeling of the devil at work. One of the many troubles with Hollywood studios today is that they allow accountants to choose the area where the film is to be made. Damn little thought is given to the historical significance!"

Brynner attended a special Hollywood screening of *Le Testament d'Orphée.* Midway through the film the audience, composed largely of high-ranking motion picture executives, started booing and hissing. Yul ordered the projectionist to cease running it. Then he hopped on the stage and shouted, "Cocteau was right when he told me that this movie should be forbidden to imbeciles!"

This diatribe didn't prevent him from being hired by MGM for *Solomon and Sheba* (1959). As bad as many of his films were, none rivaled this big-budget flop. It is well up on lists of the worst movies ever made. Yul's friend Tyrone Power had originally been selected for the leading role. When Power suffered a fatal heart attack, Brynner agreed to substitute. Because he arrived on the set after the film was in production he didn't have sufficient time to learn his lines. The result was that he often looked as if he were reading them from cue cards—as he was. "But it really didn't matter," he said. "Even by Hollywood standards the script was ludicrous."

In ancient Israel a dying King David weakly proclaims his younger son Solomon (Brynner) as his successor. Solomon's older brother Adonijah (George Sanders), a power-hungry villain, is bitter over the decision and vows to grab the throne for himself. The Egyptians become aware of the animosity and plan to attack. They are aided by the beautiful Queen of Sheba (Gina Lollobrigida), who proposes to weaken Solomon by seducing him. She arrives in a chariot that resembles a Ford convertible and projects in strong body language. Solomon is smitten. He has to be reminded to stop staring at the jewel in her navel and to engage in battle.

The movie had many absurd lines. Among them:

> Solomon: *From the first, I knew that behind those lovely green eyes is the brain of a very clever woman who would never have traveled thousands of leagues without a purpose.*
>
> Sheba: *You have found me out! How could I ever have hoped to deceive you?*
>
> Solomon: *Every woman demands a price from a man. What is yours?*

Nobody liked the movie, least of all Brynner. It produced howls of protest from Hollywood's defenders of decency, and the critics who were usually kind to Yul issued a torrent of negative reviews. The editor of a Maryland weekly newspaper was so distressed that he voiced his agony in a front-page editorial. He wrote, "Why has Yul Brynner allowed this to happen? If it was money he needed, I would have gladly pawned my typewriter or kidnapped the local banker. He should have told us he was so desperate."

A few weeks after the film was released, Yul was asked by Harold Hayes, the editor of *Esquire* magazine, to write an article about atrocious movies. (He accepted the assignment but never completed it.) When he left the *Esquire* office he stopped for lunch at a nearby French restaurant. Yul was in the midst of ordering when a tiny, frail-looking woman approached his table. Poking him on the head, she said, "Your *Solomon and Sheba* should be renamed *What Price Crap!*"

Brynner was about to shoo her away when he realized the intruder was Dorothy Parker, the well-known author of flippant short stories and satirical light verse. Instead of being annoyed he invited her to join him. For the next two hours they consumed vast amounts of Scotch, smoked dozens of cigarettes, and quoted rhymes. She particularly liked one that he had just composed:

> *Necessity teaches hungry women to be whores,*
> *And politicians to pretend to be doers.*

Yul had made another conquest. "He's the sexiest man I've ever met," Parker told her friends. Hollywood never had a hero quite like him. Few actors so captured the country's imagination. Studios, aware of the tremendous impact he had on women, kept giving him passionate, ultramasculine roles. Although he protested that he was being typed, he continued to accept them. That winter he flew to London to appear with Kay Kendall, wife of Rex Harrison, in *Once More With Feeling* (1960). It was a romantic comedy about a volatile, ill-humored symphony director and his long-suffering common-law wife.

In the early weeks of filming, Kendall collapsed on the set. She was rushed to the hospital, where doctors said she needed transfusions. Yul donated blood and insisted that other cast members do the same. The production was halted, and the delay cost the studio more than $300,000. When several Columbia executives wanted to replace her, Brynner issued an ultimatum: "If she goes, I go!" Kay stayed.

When she returned twelve pounds lighter, he tried to fatten her up with quarts of his homemade yogurt. But this time his concern wasn't sufficient. Kay died of leukemia several weeks before the film was released. Asked about her death, he said, "It's enough to make you a bloody atheist. Here was a lovely, talented woman taken away long before her time and packs of s.o.b.'s continue to run around breathing."

Yul was promptly cast in a similar romantic vehicle: *Surprise Package* (1960). This time he played Nico March, an American gangster boss who has been deported to a barren, dreary Greek island. His former underworld associates realize how disconsolate he is. They send him a surprise present— a fast-talking, beautiful blonde (Mitzi Gaynor). Despite being based on a book by Art Buchwald and having Noël Coward in the cast, *Surprise Package* was a tasteless mess.

But the time spent making the film wasn't completely in vain. Brynner discovered a voluptuous Greek extra who possessed even more alluring measurements. He frequently invited her into his dressing room—and locked the door.

Two months later, Brynner underwent a complete metamorphosis. His career took an upswing as he was cast as a western gunslinger in *The Magnificent Seven* (1960), a remake of a Japanese film classic, *Seven Samurai*. Instead of Oriental warriors, Hollywood substituted seven cowboy desperadoes.

In *The Magnificent Seven* Yul is the leader of professional frontier mercenaries who can't find work because of the inroads of law and order. They are reduced to taking low-paying jobs in a remote Mexican village that has been invaded by a band of cutthroats. During the early part of the filming, Brynner took Steve McQueen—one of the seven—under his wing. "Always try to play a bastard with a heart of gold," he told him. McQueen said it was the best advice he ever received.

While on location Brynner met twenty-seven-year-old Doris Kleiner, a slim and lovely French fashion house executive who was visiting friends. "I thought love at first sight was for schoolboys," Yul said. "But from the moment I spotted her something inside of me went zing!"

Doris, whose photograph constantly appeared in European society columns, had been born in Zagred, Yugoslavia. Her family emigrated to Chile before World War II. Later they moved to Paris, where she was employed by designer Pierre Cardin. Unlike Yul's previous affairs, this one, Virginia realized, was serious. Just before the movie was completed she went to Juarez, Mexico, and charged him with incompatibility. She received a large financial settlement and custody of Rocky.

Before the week was out Yul had traded marriage vows with Doris. They were married in a simple ceremony in Mexico City. After a swim at his rented villa in Cuernavaca, they hosted a gala party for 300 movie people. While Doris cut the wedding cake, which was decorated with delicate hearts and cupids, Yul proposed a toast. "To marriage," he said solemnly. "The finest institution the world has ever known."

He was interrupted by a tipsy film star who remarked that the tiny bridegroom figure on top of the cake had hair on his head. "Are you sure it's you?" he asked.

Brynner handled the drunk smoothly. "See what a wonderful bride can do?" he said. "Already she has made my hair grow." The guests laughed nervously, fearing a scuffle. Yul eased the tension by quoting a gypsy proverb: "It is quieter to sleep alone, but warmer to sleep with a partner."

Since most of Doris' work was in Paris, they decided to settle there. They leased a large penthouse apartment near the Arc de Triomphe. However, several weeks after the wedding, Yul and his new bride flew to California, where he started his own movie-producing company. It was called Alciona, which means peaceful in Greek. He negotiated an impressive distributing contract with United Artists—they agreed to invest $25 million for eleven Brynner movies. The

"I'm a firm believer in matrimony," Yul said. Actress Virginia Gilmore was wife number one.

Wide World

"Many fine actresses have played Anna," Yul said. "But for me there will always be only one—Gertrude Lawrence!"

Wide World

In Cecil B. DeMille's epic, *The Ten Commandments*, Yul was cast as Pharaoh Rameses I and Anne Baxter as Nefretiti, the most beautiful woman in all of Egypt.

He won an Oscar for the screen version of *The King and I*. Deborah Kerr, his co-star, felt he should have won an additional award for Best Director.

"Yul was the most talented man I've ever worked with," Deborah Kerr said.

Yul enjoyed filming *Anastasia* because Ingrid Bergman was his co-star. "It brought her back to the American screen after that ridiculous Stromboli affair," he said. "So what if she bore a child out of wedlock? That was her business!"

In *Anastasia*, besides Ingrid Bergman, he had another prominent leading lady—Helen Hayes. Both agreed that he was chiefly responsible for the movie's outstanding success.

Yul objected to playing romantic leads. When he wooed Maria Schell in *The Brothers Karamazov,* he said, "Show me a perpetual theatrical swain, and I'll show you a frustrated actor."

In *The Journey*, Yul was cast as a compassionate Soviet army officer. He allowed Deborah Kerr to escape to freedom. A critic said, "He is the sort of Russian you'd expect him to be."

"I could make my living by photographing children," Yul said. It wasn't an idle boast. Many of his pictures appeared in *Life* and other national magazines.

Solomon and Sheba is well up on lists of the worst movies ever made. Yul had to be reminded to stop staring at the jewel in Gina Lollobrigida's naval and to engage in battle.

Yul appeared with Kay Kendall and Gregory Ratoff in *Once More With Feeling*. He was devastated when Kay, wife of his friend, Rex Harrison, died from leukemia shortly before the film was released.

Having Noël Coward in the cast of *Surprise Package* failed to help. Reviewers called the movie, "Witless...Foolish...Nonsensical."

The Magnificent Seven was a remake of a Japanese classic, *Seven Samuri*. Instead of Oriental warriors, Hollywood used seven western gunslingers. Brynner was the cynical leader.

In *Teras Bulba*, Yul was cast as a scowling cossak who is feared by all men and loved by all women.

Five days after his first divorce he married Doris Kleiner, a Paris fashion house executive.

When gossip columnists referred to him as, "America's newest sex symbol," his response was, "For once they are right!"

Wife number three was Jacqueline de Thion de la Chaume de Croisset, an editor of the French edition of *Vogue* magazine.

Yul and Jacqueline adopted two Vietnamese orphans, Mia and Melody.

In *Invitation to a Gunfighter,* Brynner played a mysterious, dandified hired killer. While waiting to engage in his profession he quoted poetry, sang Creole chansons, pursued the ladies, and won at poker.

Cinema audiences were given two Brynners in *The Double Man*—Slater, a CIA agent and Kalmar, a Russian imposter. After roughing up Britt Ekland, Slater emerged victorious.

In *The Mad Woman of Chaillot*, Yul had a bit part as the chairman of the board of high-powered villains who wanted to commit Katharine Hepburn to a mental institution.

In *Westworld*, a science-fiction film, Yul played a robot lawman who is controlled by a computer. "Only a machine could knock me out," he boasted.

Kathy Lee, the 24-year-old lead dancer in the final revival of *The King and I* was wife number four. She, too, possessed the marital qualities he insisted upon: *Brains and Beauty*.

Brynner was aware that he was dying, but refused to reveal how serious his condition really was. "Why make my friends worry?" he said.

deal was halted when he called a top UA executive "an ignorant money grubber."

Yul insisted that he didn't need to earn his living by acting or directing. "I'm an expert photographer," he said. "I could earn my keep that way." His assessment of his picture-taking ability may have been quite accurate. During the shooting of *The Ten Commandments* and *The King and I*, many of the photographs he took were featured in national magazines. *Life* ran ten of them in one of its issues.

"I've been interested in photography ever since I attended a Mexican bullfight many years ago," he said. "At the time I was fooling around with a Brownie-type box camera. I was clicking away when the bull turned on the matador and gored him to death. A newspaper editor standing next to me wanted to buy the picture even before I removed it from my camera. That picture turned out to be a masterpiece. I kept that ten-dollar check for the longest time. Now, I have a $3,000 darkroom and dozens of high-priced foreign cameras and powerful lenses."

Yul didn't, however, pursue a career in photography. He returned to freelance acting and in 1962, he made *Escape From Zahrain*, a pallid Arab adventure film, for Paramount. Pearl Buck, the American novelist who had won a Nobel prize for one of her books about China, was asked to assist in the writing. She refused. "I'm much too busy," she said. "But I've been his devoted fan ever since I saw him in *The King and I* on Broadway. It would have been so nice to meet him in person. And it would have been such a simple way to earn a large sum. The studio was so eager to star him, they were willing to settle for any kind of garbage."

Sal Mineo, who appeared with Brynner in *Escape From Zahrain*, talked about him shortly before his tragic death. "I was thirteen years old when I went on as the crown prince in the stage production of *The King and I*. First I was an understudy. For more than a year I used to watch him from the wings. He looked so stern in his makeup. Other members of the cast told me that he had a keen sense of humor, but I found it hard to believe. Anyone who played the king so ruthlessly couldn't possibly have one.

"To play the crown prince, I had to wear Oriental makeup. Since I didn't know how to apply it, I decided to ask him. My knees literally shook when I knocked on his door. When he saw me, he said, 'Hiya, Sal.' I was floored that he knew my name. I forgot every word of what I had planned to say. But I didn't have to tell him—somehow he had found out. He told me to sit down in front of his dressing table. I was too frightened to move. That's when he said, 'Frankly, I don't see how makeup can help you.' He laughed. I laughed. His joke broke the ice.

"After that we became good friends. Even though he was many years older, I considered him my friend. He always talked to me as an equal, never down to me. At one point I told him that I was having trouble with my part. Another adult might have said, 'You're just imagining it!' He didn't. Instead he said that I wasn't playing it straight enough. He suggested that we get together to rehearse it. He was that way with every kid in the show.

"One time a very little Chinese girl in the cast mispronounced a word. Instead of saying, 'I don't understand it?' she said, 'I don't *underworld* it?' All the other kids howled. Yul picked her up, kissed her, and told us, 'If the underworld was filled with such lovely little girls like this one, it would probably be renamed overworld.' I remember I went away thinking that if I'd had a teacher like Mr. Brynner, I'd never have cut school. He could be gruff with older people, but never with us.

"When we made *Escape From Zahrain*, I could tell right off that the years hadn't changed him in his attitude toward children. One of the other actors in the movie had a six-year-old son. Several times the boy visited the set. He became quite attached to Yul—and for a very good reason. Everyone else told the kid to get lost, but not him. The two of them were forever playing games. Yul would invent wonderful ones. A favorite was a kind of Johnny-On-The-Pony. Yul had renamed it Johnny-On-The-Camel. He was the camel—a singing one!"

As soon as *Escape From Zahrain* was completed, Yul co-starred with Tony Curtis in *Taras Bulba* (1962), an extravaganza that had been adapted from a novel by Nikolai Gogal. Brynner had some apprehension about the film when he learned it was to be shot in the foothills of Argentina's Andes Mountains instead of the Russian Steppes. He became more concerned when he discovered how much the original story had been altered. There was, however, some compensation. Argentine schoolgirls lined the streets as Yul drove to work. They chanted, "Y-U-L! Y-U-L!" A toy manufacturer fashioned a baldheaded doll that closely resembled the actor, and a cocktail named "The Yul" became the country's leading alcoholic drink. It consisted of a mound of shaved ice and straight vodka, topped with a plastic rose petal.

His dressing room, a converted large Mack truck, resembled a covered wagon. The outstanding piece of furniture was an immense couch upholstered in red-striped linen. A newspaper in Buenos Aires took a photograph of it. The caption read: "Brynner and company slept here."

Yul was furious when the picture appeared. "There is only one woman in my life," he said. "And that is my wife!" When he learned that Doris was pregnant, they moved from Paris to Switzerland, where they rented a house on Lake Geneva. "We figured it was a good place to raise a child," he said. "As soon as the doctor showed me my new daughter, I fastened my eyes on the loveliest sight I'd ever seen— she was truly beautiful. We named her Victoria. I don't want to appear to be prejudiced, but she is one of the most exquisite-looking females in the world."

Most of Brynner's close friends were Europeans. "They're much more civilized abroad," he told reporters. "They live and let live. Europeans don't ask you what line of work you're in or about your religion or how much you have in the bank. They allow some privacy. That's much more than you do!"

He was particularly averse to American columnists. When one asked him whether he wore pajamas to bed or slept in the nude, he glowered at him and said, "Neither the press nor anyone reading about me is about to enjoy the privilege of sleeping with me, so I see no reason why I have to reveal my bedtime habits!"

Sheila Graham, a well-known Hollywood writer, accused him of being the most egotistical actor she'd ever met. "He once claimed that I had written something about him that was untrue," she said. " 'Why didn't you check with me first?' he shouted. I replied, 'But you move around so much I never know where you are.' I'm still shocked when I recall his reply. He said, 'All you had to do was pick up the phone, ask for Switzerland, and tell the operator you want to talk to Yul Brynner. Even if I'm not at home, she'd know where to find me.'

"I know Switzerland is not a very large country, but really!"

The following year, Yul, Doris, and Victoria flew to the Orient. He had agreed to appear in a United Artists film, *Flight From Ashiya* (1964). As Sergeant Mike Takashima, a gung-ho Japanese-Polish paratrooper, he helps in a daring rescue mission. The most dramatic scene occurred off camera. One of the actors referred to a Japanese bit player as a "slant-eyed bastard." Brynner overheard the insult and promptly slugged the offender. He refused to continue until an apology was made.

During the filming he learned about John Kennedy's

assassination. He was very upset by the President's death. When Yul wasn't required to be in front of the camera he would retire to his dressing room, where he'd pace the floor and gulp large amounts of Scotch. The two had met when Kennedy was a young congressman from Massachusetts. They both had been invited to a large, formal dinner party in Washington, D.C., that was given by Alice Longworth, daughter of Theodore Roosevelt. Kennedy's bow tie had come loose, and Brynner showed him how to knot it properly.

When dinner was finished, the male guests retired to the library, where Yul was the center of attraction. The men were intrigued when he started discussing his theories about life and death. Brynner told them that he had grown up with an Oriental philosophy on the subject, that he lived with the idea that you go to bed not knowing if you had a tomorrow. "Jack kept peppering me with questions," he said. "After that night we became good friends."

Yul's schedule was a full one. As soon as *Flight From Ashiya* was completed, he starred in *Invitation to a Gunfighter* (1964). He was cast as Jules Gaspart D'Estaing, a mysterious, dandified New Orleans gunslinger who is hired to do some killing. While he waits for the psychological moment he recites French poetry, sings Creole chansons, and charms all the ladies.

Franklin Henderson, the movie's comptroller recalled, "In every scene he was in he was required to present a machismo sexiness. Over and over he was told to play a western version of the character he made famous in *The King and I*. 'Only make him more sophisticated,' we'd say. We never let him forget it. That was our mistake. We should have known that he'd ignore our instruction. He conducted a one-man mutiny—ripped up thick scripts into tiny bits and tossed them around like so much confetti. It was the same with the props. When he disagreed, nothing was sacred. But midway during the shooting his wrath seemed to evaporate. He had just learned that in his next picture he would costar with Marlon Brando."

About a dozen reporters were on hand to cover the historical meeting of the two giant stars. They watched Marlon put his hands in his pockets as he spotted Brynner. He nodded slightly and mumbled a halfhearted greeting. Yul did exactly the same thing. Their conversation was dominated by sighs and deep breaths until suddenly, the two actors started laughing. They then admitted that the entire episode had been a prearranged joke. Their buffoonery continued in a joint press conference:

> Brando: *Yul, you are the screen's finest actor.*
> Brynner: *No, no, Marlon. That title belongs solely to you. You alone!*
> Brando: *You are being much too modest!*
> Brynner: *I guess that's my failing. That quality of being humble has plagued me all my life.*
> Brando: *I know just what you mean. I, too, suffer from that affliction.*
> Brynner: *Let's bravely face the fact that we have to travel down life's path being two misguided wallflowers.*

Yul wasn't known for handing out compliments. It was quite different in Brando's case. "I regard him as one of the finest living performers," he said. "Working alongside him will be a pleasurable learning experience."

During the shooting of *The Saboteur: Code Name—Morituri* (1965), the two stars often engaged in long and involved conversations on the state of the world. Near the end of the filming one of the cameramen was called a Communist because he had been discovered reading a copy of Mao Tsetung's little *Red Book*, a compilation of the Chinese leader's political sayings. Both Brynner and Brando defended the man's rights. "He should be allowed to read whatever he wants," Yul said. "But as for me, I wouldn't keep that bloody trash in my library."

He classified himself as a "vocal free-thinking anti-Communist imbued with a righteous passion for all minorities." He said he had refused to play Stalin in a movie. "Over the years I've portrayed many tyrants," he said. "I tried and believe succeeded in getting across some understanding, some sympathy for those roles. In Stalin's case, no. He was a bastard, all right. But he didn't have a heart of gold. Nohow!"

The Saboteur failed to excite the reviewers, who seemed to agree with Bosley Crowther of *The New York Times*. "It is beyond interest and concern," the veteran critic wrote.

"So what if it's a bit cheesy," Yul said. "The reviewers should realize they are looking at a classic. Just having Brynner and Brando together is reason enough for raves!"

– CHAPTER SEVEN –

More
Screen
Disasters

BRYNNER hoped to regain some of his lost cinema prestige by appearing in a United Nations-sponsored documentary that attacked the easy availability of narcotics. Joining two dozen other international stars—among them Marcello Mastroianni, Anthony Quale, Omar Sharif, Trevor Howard, Jean-Claude Pascal, and Princess Grace of Monaco—he took a small role in *The Poppy is Also a Flower* (1966).

"Not only did he offer his services," said Gilbert Roland, who was also in the film, "but he kept popping up on television publicizing the idea. It got so that you couldn't switch the dial without hearing him sound off. He was instrumental in getting most of us to volunteer. I think we each got a token payment of a dollar—it was his idea. No one could refuse him—until you said yes he'd keep on with his wheedling."

But despite Yul's good intentions, most critics felt *The Poppy is Also a Flower* was heavyhanded old-fashioned melodrama. Several weeks later he accepted another bit part in *Cast a Giant Shadow* (1966). This time he played a Jewish resistance leader who helps create the state of Israel. Here, too, he did some proselytizing. Between takes he'd sit on his custom-made chair and hold forth on the evils of anti-Semitism. Luther Adler, one of the actors in the picture, said,

"He knew more about the subject than most rabbis. When I asked him about it, he told me that because of his gypsy background he was well aware of what it was like to be persecuted. True or not, he always had an answer for everything. Once he lectured me for more than an hour on Einstein's theory of relativity. Later, I checked up on what he had said. You know what? He was dead right!"

During the shooting, a Hollywood fan magazine reported that Yul and Marilyn Monroe had been involved in a torrid love affair. Not surprisingly, Brynner didn't deny or confirm the story. However, his reply did give the impression that Monroe had been one of his conquests—maybe!

"I'm flattered," he said. "All I can say is that Marilyn has good taste in her escorts. She is an attractive and sensitive woman. When she puts on her warpaint she instantly becomes a radiant thing. She can also look like an old pancake left over from a Sunday breakfast. But I haven't got time to discuss her. There's another matter I have to attend to."

Eighteen years before, he had attained United States citizenship. Now, he decided to relinquish it. "Giving it up is a mere formality," he said. "Doris and my daughter Victoria are Swiss subjects. I have dual citizenship—U.S. and Swiss. Don't blame me if I want to normalize my family life. Not to take the chance of being separated from them in case of an international crisis. I don't think that I have to prove my loyalty and devotion to the United States. Yet, some bloody fools are implying that my motives are purely monetary."

Ed Sullivan had called Yul a hypocritical ingrate. He said that Brynner "takes our money and then runs off to Switzerland. I say they can keep him." Yul had to be constrained from hiring demonstrators to picket Sullivan's apartment house. To show how much affection he had for the United States, he accepted the American ambassador's invitation to attend a Fourth of July celebration that was to be held later in the week in Tel Aviv.

He was the only one of the original band of gunfighters to appear in *Return of the Seven* (1966), a successor to *The Magnificent Seven*. Once again he donned his black cowboy costume and resumed the role of Chris, a mysterious shoot-to-kill philosopher-gunslinger. Yul urged Steve McQueen, whom he regarded as his protegé, to also repeat his part. McQueen begged off because of another commitment. "I'd sure like to," he said. "But I'm too busy." Privately, he admitted the new plot was absurd.

At a party given by Jack Benny and Mary Livingston, Brynner and McQueen insisted on serenading the guests with a medley of cowboy ballads. They both had been drinking heavily, and when it came time to leave they began whistling for their horses. They were disappointed when their chauffeur-driven automobiles appeared in the driveway.

"Where's mah horse?" Yul asked drunkenly.

"Thar must be a horsethief in th' crowd," McQueen replied.

He had promised Yul that he would appear with him in his next movie. A month later Brynner signed a contract to star in *Triple Cross* (1967), a spy thriller that was to be made in England and France. Again, McQueen reneged. This time, he offered his excuse in a cablegram: "I'M TRULY SORRY THAT I CAN'T BE WITH YOU BUT MY HORSE REFUSES TO SWIM THE ATLANTIC."

"Even without Steve, I enjoyed making *Triple Cross*," Yul said. "It was good fun, providing you didn't take it seriously. The movie was a spoof of cloak-and-dagger stories that were immensely popular in the sixties. I was cast as a German baron who was a high-ranking army officer. Naturally, I had to wear a monocle."

When his wife Doris and four-year-old Victoria visited

him on the set, "My daughter would take one look at me wearing that silly monocle and burst out laughing," Brynner recalled. "I tried not to react, but I suppose my feelings were hurt."

Victoria was a startling beauty, and Yul found it difficult to be strict with her. He was once on a radio talk show with Dr. Benjamin Spock, the pediatrician. The two discussed permissiveness. "Ben told me," Brynner said, "that a parent who is wishy-washy is too often a noncaring parent. One moment the child is yelled at for being destructive and then for the exact transgression is patted and kissed. Doris and I decided not to make that mistake."

Cinema audiences were treated to two Yul Brynners in *The Double Man* (1968). One is Dan Slater, an audacious CIA agent who is investigating the mysterious death of his son. The other is a crafty Soviet impostor. When Allen Dulles, the former head of the CIA, saw the movie, he remarked, "If one of my agents made so many errors, I'd personally fire him. As a rule I like suspense movies, but this one deserved to be stored in the bottom of the barrel."

The Double Man was supposed to have taken place in the Austrian Alps. Instead, some scenes were shot in England during the summer months. Yul rebelled when fake snow had to be used and threatened to walk off the set, but nothing came of it. When asked why he hadn't followed through, he said, "I have a wonderful nature of forgetting things in a hurry."

In his next screen venture, *Villa Rides* (1968), Yul was cast as Pancho Villa, the famous Mexican revolutionary. Soon after the film was released, Arthur Godfrey read a rhyming review on his NBC television program:

Villa Rides is filled with so much rot,
Authentic Mexican history it is not.

So what else has this wacky movie got?
Yul. And these days he's not so hot.

Brynner was in a Paris hotel when he was told about Godfrey's uncomplimentary appraisal. He stayed up all night composing a rebuttal. As soon as it was finished he sent it to NBC and demanded equal time.

"I'd served a hitch in the Navy, and I thought nothing could embarrass me," Godfrey said. "But I have to admit that I blushed when I read Yul's reply. Practically every other word was obscene."

Brynner defended *Villa Rides*. "It was a wonderful screenplay," he said. "The director whom I had personally approved had to bow out because he was needed on another film. He was replaced with a director who had very little movie experience. When it came out, everything looked flattened and the performances were meaningless. Added to that sorry mess, the film had been cut in the wrong way. It was a bloody shame, because it's so rare to get a good script. Damn few picture makers really know anything about the film industry. To get a cushy movie job you have to be an accountant, a lawyer, or a stockbroker. It's very uncommon to have risen from the ranks!"

Brynner preferred making movies outside the United States. "Foreign countries still regard the actor as a somebody," he said. "In Hollywood the actor has become just another businessman—seldom a true artist."

He was pleased when he signed a contract to star in a film that was to be made in Yugoslavia, *The Battle on the River Neretva* (1968). The budget for the movie was $10 million—at the time the highest ever given to a film from an Eastern European country other than the Soviet Union. Brynner played a demolition expert who, with his fellow partisans, stubbornly resists occupation of his homeland.

Still doing his own stunts, he was nearly killed while running across a bridge. Explosive charges were going off all around him. One was detonated too early and nearly blew him off the bridge. He managed to cling to a steel post. When Orson Welles, who was also in the film, heard about the near fatality he told Brynner, "I guess your time hasn't come yet. Like me, you can continue to provoke people." (Welles died on the same day Yul did.)

Yul's notices improved when he appeared in *The Madwoman of Chaillot* (1969) as one of Katharine Hepburn's persecutors. He was part of a group of high-powered villains who want to commit the eccentric woman to a mental institution. She had discovered their plan to transform Paris into a giant oilfield with petroleum-pumping derricks on the Champs Elysees.

"The script called for me to be mean to Katie," he said. "That's an almost impossible task. But I was helped when she scolded me. On the very first day of shooting I had given her a shiny new bicycle. She was riding it when I attempted to snap her picture. She wasn't having any of it and started bawling me out. I felt just like I was a little boy doing something naughty. However, after that it was a little easier to be spiteful to her."

The Madwoman of Chaillot had been a successful Broadway play, which Yul felt accounted for its superiority. Although his part was small and he had a great deal of competition, he was singled out for his performance. Hepburn was surrounded by an outstanding cast: Charles Boyer, Dame Edith Evans, Danny Kaye, Margaret Leighton, Oscar Homolka, Claude Dauphan, Richard Chamberlain. One critic called Yul's performance "Gilt-edged . . . too bad it's so brief."

Briefer still was the fifty-three-second cameo role Yul had in *The Magic Christian* (1970). Not listed in the screen credits, he was cloaked in a chic, tight-fitting evening gown, lipsticked, and decorously coiffeured. In a lilting falsetto he sang "Mad About the Boy." Then pulling off the wig he revealed his true identity.

"I teased him about appearing in drag," said his friend Jean Levin. "And I wasn't the only one. I still chuckle when I recall what he did to prove his masculinity. Soon after the movie was shown in Paris theaters, he flew to New York on Air France. I knew one of the stewardesses who personally witnessed this event. Yul and a blonde Scandinavian actress were fellow passengers in the first-class section. They got real *sympatique* after drinking lots of champagne. When she made for the lavatory he followed her. The occupied light was on for a long time. Finally, they came out. As the plane neared New York, my friend, the stewardess, asked him if everything on the flight had been okay. 'I guess so,' Yul replied. 'But that damned lavatory is much too small!' "

The actress Yvonne de Carlo once attested to his masculinity when she said of him, "He makes you so weak that you're immediately drawn to him. It's not what he says, but how he says it. He has that unknown quality that makes you instantly want to surrender."

Near the end of the year, Yul traveled once again to Yugoslavia to play a Cossack captain in *Romance of a Horsethief* (1971), a fanciful tale about hard-riding, hard-loving Jews. The plot was about Jewish peasants of Malava, a small border town, who made their living by horsetrading and horse stealing.

"The studio intended the picture to be a lighthearted comedy," Brynner said, "but discovered that there was nothing funny between Jews and Cossacks. I did, however, get to drive around in a beautiful shiny black Mercedes limousine. The only other one like it belonged to Marshal Tito. Sometimes his guards would get us mixed up."

One morning Yul was sitting in the back seat of his car when four motorcycle policemen pulled up and escorted him to the set. Several nights later he met Tito at an embassy reception. When he told the Communist leader about the mistake, Tito remarked, "Those policemen give me a wonderful idea. Let's trade places."

"No, thanks," Yul replied quickly. "It would be a comedown for me. You see, I've been a king!"

In September of 1970, Brynner revisited Broadway as a spectator. He was an extremely proud parent as he watched his twenty-three-year-old son appear in *Opium*, a one-man show. In addition to Rock's being the play's sole character, the young man had translated and adapted it from a diary kept by his godfather, Jean Cocteau. For two hours, Yul carefully observed his son wage a bitter but determined battle against a demon that was destroying him. When the final curtain came down he joined the audience in enthusiastic applause. He kept a copy of Clive Barnes' *New York Times* review in his wallet and proudly displayed it to everyone he met. The theater critic had written that Rock's performance was "fascinating."

Young Brynner had developed into a taller edition of his father. He had the same penetrating voice, magnetic brown eyes, and a narrow face dominated by strong cheekbones, as well as the same self-confidence.

Yul defended continuing his association with European filmmakers by saying, "Some of their sleepers are very worthwhile." And early the following year, he appeared in *Light at the Edge of the World* (1971). It didn't turn out to be one of the sleepers he had been talking about. The movie was supposed to be based on a Jules Verne adventure novel, but any similarity was purely accidental. His costars were Kirk Douglas and Samantha Eggar.

"Although I'll admit that the original story had been butchered," Yul said, "the critics ignored some of the superb scenes. Especially the one where Kirk and I have a confrontation on top of a burning lighthouse. In its own way it was a little masterpiece. Professor Chekhov frequently lectured us on superfluous speeches not being necessary—they would lead you astray. I've always remembered that advice. But the director, a newcomer to the field, wanted us to talk the action. I disagreed. In that scene, Kirk and I said very little. It was obvious, however, from our facial expressions and body movements, just how we felt. Words were unessential. I wanted more silence instead of that silly dialogue. The director refused to take my advice."

Brynner's next role was a laconic soldier of fortune in a spaghetti Western called *Adios Sabata* (1971). The movie was short on plot but long on violence—a goldplated, sawed-off repeating rifle and a triple-barreled derringer got a great deal of practice. Yul made good use of both of them.

Alberto Grimaldi, the producer, had loaned him a sleek cherry-red convertible to ferry him to and from the set. Initially, Brynner made the trip in half an hour. Each day he managed to reduce his time. He had it down to twenty-one minutes when the car got out of control and crashed into a stone embankment. Fortunately, Yul wasn't hurt. However, the car was reduced to rubble. When he requested that it be replaced with another sports car, he was told that it would be best if he was driven by a chauffeur.

"Yul gave me his version of the accident," Jean Levin said. "According to him it was entirely the automobile's fault—defective breaks. In all the years I knew him, never once did he take the blame for anything. It was always somebody else's fault. Even the breakup of his marriage wasn't due to something he did. He and Doris were having lots of marital problems. I suppose the chief one was his continued interest in other women."

Brynner and Levin were dining at Maxim's in Paris just before Yul was divorced for the second time. "He looked wretched," his friend recalled. "I asked him what was the matter. He just stared at me. Then he finally said, 'The more years I'm married the less I understand matrimony.' He seemed so unhappy that I was positive he'd never go through it again. But sure enough, he soon took another bride."

Wife number three was thirty-four-year-old Jacqueline de Thion de la Chaume de Croisset, a fashion editor of the French edition of *Vogue*. She was the widow of a publishing executive who had died in an automobile crash. Before that she had been briefly married to a French doctor. She had a teenage daughter.

"I kept running into Jacqueline at Paris cocktail parties," Yul said. "She was the most aristocratically stunning woman I'd ever met. *Soigné* and witty—a delightful combination."

They were married in Deauville, France, on September 23, 1971. One of the witnesses gave Brynner a motorcycle for a wedding present. "He was really resourceful," Yul said. "Gave it to me a day before the ceremony so that if I wanted to make a hasty departure, I could. But I certainly didn't want to back out. I'm a firm believer in marriage. After all, I was married to Virginia for sixteen years, and eleven years to Doris. That should be proof enough how highly I regard it."

Jacqueline preferred to continue to live in France. He obliged her by purchasing a fifty-five-acre estate in Normandy that was called "La Manion de Criquebeuf." Baron Guy de Rothschild was his neighbor. "I'm very fortunate to have that place," Yul said. "It's really a treasure. Every room, even the bathrooms, have fireplaces. The land is covered with apple and pear trees. When I'm there I chop wood, raise doves—and just sit and watch the grass grow. That place helps me renew myself.

"These days the world is so full of haste and worry, people desperately need an oasis. I don't mean to imply that you must buy a wildly expensive house and grounds to get that feeling. No, not at all. When I was poor I had a special tree in a crowded Greenwich Village park that put me in the same mood. Whenever I sat under it I felt that I was in some remote Shangri-la."

He was reluctant to leave his new home, but CBS convinced him to costar with Samantha Eggar in a weekly television series based on *The King and I*. It was to be one of the most expensive undertakings in TV history.

"The shooting had to be postponed five times," Brynner said. "Members of the cast got sick, the set burned down, it rained so hard that no one could get to the studio. That should have been a warning. But CBS was determined to go ahead. It was a big mistake, because the series had to be canceled after eight episodes."

Before Yul left the United States he agreed to appear with Burt Reynolds and Raquel Welch in *Fuzz* (1972), a comedy-melodrama that was about to be filmed in Boston. He was cast as a sinister saboteur who threatens to blow up the multimillionaire mayor's wife and daughter unless he's paid $500,000. To prove he means business, he disposes of the deputy mayor by planting a bomb in his limousine.

"The movie may not have set box-office records," said Reynolds, "but it was well worth the price of an admission ticket just to watch Yul perform. He was a thoroughgoing pro. Every time he completed a scene I wanted to applaud —he was that good."

Brynner had better luck in his next venture, *Westworld* (1973). The film was written and directed by Michael Crichton, the author of the best-selling novel *The Andromeda Strain*. "It was Crichton's first venture into movie directing, and he was more than a little nervous," Yul recalled. "He sought my advice on how I planned to play the leading role. 'You can do it any way you want,' he said. 'Like Gary Cooper in *High Noon*, or like Hank Fonda in *My Darling Clementine*, or like Jack Palance in *Shane*.' So I said, 'Why not like Yul Brynner in *The Magnificent Seven*?' It turned out that Crichton had hoped I would say that, but hadn't wanted to suggest it in case I turned it down. He thought I wouldn't want to do a repeat. But this was entirely different, because it was about a robot whose characterization was based on Yul Brynner."

Reviews were favorable, with most critics agreeing that he had given a good performance. One of them said, "Brynner was an excellent robot. It was a gamble but he won out. His tongue may have been in his cheek but it showed not."

Yul was pleased that his mechanical-man role was well received. "It was good to read those sensible notices," he said. "I should have retired from motion pictures after that one. I could see the handwriting on the wall. Moviemakers, even the foreign ones, had begun catering to a new audience mainly composed of smart young know-it-alls."

Instead of doing what he should have done, buoyed by those favorable reviews he agreed to play another robot in *Futureworld* (1975), a superficial sequel to *Westworld*, which one reviewer said "was as much fun as running barefoot through Astroturf." And later that same year Brynner played a gangster leader in *The Ultimate Warrior* (1975), a grade C movie about a mobster who rules New York in the year 2012 until the poisoned atmosphere forces him to move his operation to an island off the Carolina coast. This time a critic wondered "if we were being fair to the South by sending it such a bomb."

On the rare occasions Yul publicly acknowledged failure, he would flash an evil grin and say, "But think of the money—a gypsy trait." Was greed the answer? Did a large bank account make him callous to insult? Or was his ego so enormous that he was impervious to it? Only *The King and I, The Ten Commandments, Anastasia, The Journey,* and *The Magnificent Seven* brought him high critical praise. Five out of thirty-nine is a poor shooting score.

Some of his lemons had good writers, directors, producers, and actors. Why, then, were they so inferior? Three cinema stars who worked with him in several of these debacles offered explanations:

Eli Wallach: *I really don't think money was the chief factor. Yul honestly believed that his mere presence could improve a bad plot.*

James Mason: *Often, when a studio realized they were faced with a potential flop they tried to save it by calling for Brynner. He accepted the challenge. Unfortunately, the movie was doomed from the start.*

Burt Reynolds: *In this business you have to expect some clinkers. Yul simply had more than his share.*

—CHAPTER EIGHT—

A
United Nations
Diplomat

YUL was elated when he was appointed a special consultant to the United Nations High Command for Refugees. Although he was unsalaried he was so eager to lend a hand that he'd be up the entire night making plans.

He thought of applying for a Guggenheim Fellowship. "Of course I wouldn't take the money," he said hastily. "But that desperate situation needed all the publicity it could get. Just think of the free exposure: 'Yul Brynner is awarded a Guggenheim to study displaced people.'" He abandoned the idea when the time came to begin his tour. During the late fifties and early sixties he traveled 25,000 miles by horseback, jeep, and plane to camps throughout Europe and the Middle East.

UN officials had become aware of Brynner's deep concern for the underprivileged after he had given a series of UN-sponsored concerts for Korean orphans. When he was officially named he said, "I don't intend to single-handedly eliminate the refugee problem, but before I'm through I'll sure as hell make a dent in it."

"And he certainly did!" said August Lindt, the UN High Commissioner for Refugees. "Heretofore, many celebrity visits consisted of handshaking and passing out chewing gum to the children—of course, in front of cameras. Brynner altered that picture. He lived with the refugees, ate with them, talked to them, and learned their bleak stories."

Over the years Brynner had earned a well-deserved reputation of being flip or sarcastic with reporters. That changed when he was discussing refugees. The "I" still cropped up, but the major part of each interview was devoted to the plight of displaced people he'd met in the camps. When he spoke about refugees his face took on a glow and he sounded like an old-time revivalist. The bombast was still there, but it no longer was reserved for himself. He had discovered a worthy cause and it was plain to see that he was emotionally involved and very sincere.

Yul had heard tragic tales wherever he went. In a camp near Salzburg he met Joseph Zamjski, who was literally drinking himself to death. He had been a shoemaker's apprentice in a small Polish village when he had been captured by the Germans. "With my own eyes I had seen them shoot my mother to death," he told Brynner.

"Zamjski was only forty-three years old," Yul said. "But he looked like my grandfather. His wrinkles had wrinkles. Somehow he always managed to get hold of a bottle of liquor. I could see what it was doing to him and tried to reason with him, but he just laughed in an insane sort of way. 'I know that I'll never leave this place alive,' he told me. 'But this way it makes things easier.' I knew that he was telling me the truth."

Brynner and his guitar entertained several hundred refugees in a camp near Stuttgart, West Germany. The actor squatted on the floor as he sang melodies from *The King and I*. "When I finished," he recalled, "there was a sudden hush. I couldn't hear a solitary sound. Just as I started thinking that my performance had been a complete bust, they started applauding and whistling and banging on their seats.

"I was used to all sorts of ovations, but nothing compared to that evening. It was the most exhilarating experience I've ever had. In a hovel they called a theater, I was grateful that Yul Brynner had been given talent. I realized that for a few moments I had helped those poor unfortunates forget their misery."

Renée was a ten-year-old Bedouin girl Yul met in the Gaza Strip. Matter-of-factly she told him—via a translator—that both of her parents were dead. "Fire," she said. "They got burned up when our burner exploded." She now shared a tent with her aunt, uncle, and six cousins.

"Since most of the Bedouins have always lived on next to nothing," Brynner said, "their privations didn't seem to matter. But this youngster was very different. I was used to seeing children laugh and play. She did neither—just sat and stared. When asked a question she would reply in a blank manner, as if nothing she said could possibly be of any interest.

"My heart went out to her. I thought of my own well-protected daughter. I've always had a good rapport with children. But it wasn't the case with Renée. Had I come too late?"

Also in a Gaza Strip camp he noticed one of the older men staring at him. "No matter which way I turned," Brynner said, "I could still feel his gaze. In show business it's not unusual to have people stare at you. I'm not being immodest when I say that I get more than most other celebrities. But this was different. It was as if the man was in a trance—his eyes never moved away from me.

"Finally, I asked him why he was doing it. At first he didn't reply—just kept right on staring. Then silently he pointed to the boots I was wearing. I thought there was something wrong with them, but realized that he was fascinated by the boots. That's when I took them off. I handed them to him, but he didn't understand what I was doing. When he did, the most wonderful smile appeared on his unshaven face.

I watched as he put them on. It didn't matter that they were several sizes too large. He was in eighth heaven."

On Yul's way back to the makeshift shelter he was staying in, he had to cross several muddy fields in his stockinged feet. "I didn't notice that they were soaking wet," he recalled. "I was too busy thinking how wonderful it would be if the refugee problem could be solved that easily."

In Jordan, Brynner photographed some boys playing soccer near a barbed-wire barrier. When one of the youngsters accidentally kicked the ball over the fence, he looked resigned to losing it. Brynner managed to retrieve the ball and hand it back. "You'd think I had just given each of them shiny new bikes," he said. "Later, I learned why. Anything that was found on the other side of the *rusty iron curtain* was immediately confiscated by the ever-present guards. When I talked to the boys, I was shocked by their vehemence. They spewed hatred for those they blamed for their predicament —Americans included."

Upon Brynner's return to the United States, the UN arranged a press conference. He spoke in the serious, measured tones of a man who felt deeply about his subject. When a reporter asked him about his Hollywood plans, he replied, "I suppose I should give you some meaningless jargon about how films provide much-needed refreshment to the downtrodden. But that would be a crock of horse manure. What they need is freedom to get out of the camps that were originally built for slave labor. These people are rotting away morally and physically. You and I have to get them out!"

Three Brynner efforts aimed in that direction were announced by the UN moderator. The first was Yul's book, *Bring Forth the Children*. Illustrated with photographs by Brynner and Inge Monrath, wife of playwright Arthur Miller, it emphasized his experiences among displaced youngsters. All his earnings from the book were to be donated to the UN Refugee Office.

A second event was a documentary titled *Rescue—With Yul Brynner*. It would be presented by Edward R. Murrow on CBS. And later in the month the United Nations planned to make available a thirty-minute movie, *Mission to No-Man's Land*, which had been shot during Yul's tour of the refugee camps.

Brynner's tour was acknowledged by several U.S. legislators. Senator Wayne Morse of Oregon delivered a particularly moving speech on the floor of the upper house concerning Yul's UN role, and other lawmakers, both Democrat and Republican, joined in. The entire chamber cheered when Senator Everett Dirksen of Illinois, who was known for his flowery rhetoric, said, "The actor too often deserves derision and chaffing because his love exists for only one person—himself. Yul Brynner, the luminary we are eulogizing today, may also fancy himself, and rightfully so. But in addition to any subliminal ego that's present, he had opened his heart to the world's less fortunate. His charity didn't stop with his just being aware of their wretchedness and despair. He helped. Oh, how he helped."

When Yul was told about all the extravagant praise that had come his way, he was temporarily out of words. But not for long. "Who am I to disagree with the learned senators?" he said.

In 1970 the United Nations presented him with a scroll honoring his commitment. Brynner made a brief speech when he accepted the award. The audience gave him a standing ovation when he said, "Children of all persuasions are entitled to equal freedom. Freedom to succeed. Freedom to fail. And freedom to live their lives as ordinary human beings." He couldn't resist adding, "I hope I'm remembered for my UN work, but I fear you will always think of me as that crazy actor who shaved his head clean as a billiard ball."

CHAPTER NINE

Bald Men
Are More
Sensual

GRADY Miller, Emanuel Manfretti, and Calvin Holitzer all pay homage to the memory of Yul. Each morning they repeat his name three times as they tenderly pat their hairless heads. They are among the 150 members of the *Shaved Heads Are Sexy Club*, a highly informal organization headquartered in St. Paul, Minnesota. Yul is their patron saint.

"It's not your ordinary club," said Miller, the do-nothing president. "No dues, no assessments, no meetings. Not a thing to do, but share a mutual desire to take pride in having no hair on our heads. Most of us came to that decision after seeing our King perform. I know it was that way with me. Amy, that's the wife, flipped when she saw his bald noggin in the movies."

Now and then—mostly then—they get together to fool around and swap baldheaded jokes. About ten years ago some of the members met in Key West, Florida. They asked Brynner to join them. He refused, but sent a cigar box filled with hair fuzz his electric shaver had clipped off. Plus a terse note saying that he didn't advertise his head.

He was adamant in denying that he shaved it bare in order to gain popularity. "If I thought for a minute that my success hinged on it," he snapped, "I'd cut off my whole skull! I don't care a hoot what I look like. I'm not a woman, so I can't say what makes a man interesting physically. But what makes him interesting to me is how he lives, how he dies, what he contributes while he is alive. He is not attractive because he has a certain kind of nose or a certain kind of a head. These things are merely props."

Just a prop it might be, but he continued to regularly shave his head. Executives at Proctor & Gamble were so impressed by the popularity of Brynner and his shaven head that they decided to pattern their new cleaner after his image. Mr. Clean closely resembled Yul Brynner. The actor feigned annoyance and threatened to sue, but nothing came of it.

Several large companies asked Yul to endorse their products. Among them were makers of men's underwear, swimming trunks, and an exotic brand of perfume. He spurned their offers, but was receptive when approached by the manufacturer of water-ski equipment. He was an expert water skier, having jumped eighty-five feet. He was about to accept a down payment when he was told that their ad would say: *Even a man without hair can slalom.*

"I don't exploit my head!" he shouted as he stormed out.

Dorothy Kilgallen, a popular Broadway columnist, heard about the incident. She wrote, "No matter what Yul says, he knows a good thing when he sees it. He's wise enough to realize that with a mop of hair his provocativeness might escape notice."

When a Hollywood producer suggested that he don a wig, Marlene Dietrich, his onetime close companion, said indignantly, "Covering his sensual dome is like putting clothes on Lady Godiva."

Previously, all of Hollywood's leading men sported lots of hair: Rudolph Valentino, Charles Boyer, Tyrone Power, Robert Taylor, Cary Grant. When their locks started to thin they rushed nervously to toupee artists. They knew that a luxuriant head of hair was essential for masculine appeal. No one dared to trample on the screen's longtime rule: Bald heads are for secondary character actors only!

Brynner's hair had been receding since he was in his early thirties and bald spots about the size of half-dollars began to appear. Grudgingly, he admitted that the idea of shaving his entire head for *The King and I* had "some merit."

"It was a brilliant stroke," said Milton Kuhlman, who had worked in the promotion department of Columbia Pictures. "The talk at the studio was that it added thousands of dollars to his yearly income. We once sent out pictures of him—with and without hair—to several dozen movie editors. We asked them which style they liked better. Not a single one voted for hair. They all felt that with hair he was just another good-looking face. But without any he was pure dynamite."

Kuhlman recalled that Brynner's bald head almost had another function. "It was seriously considered to serve as a teleprompter," he said. "While we were making *Once More With Feeling*, Kay Kendall, Yul's costar, had trouble remembering her lines. It was discovered that his shiny head would make a fine reflector—her lines could be beamed off it. I know it sounds crazy, but it was actually considered."

During the filming, Brynner was informed that the Hollywood Wax Museum had just moved him to the place of honor. "You have become our leading attraction," Yul was told. "When women see you they immediately want to stroke your bare head."

The wife of Grady Miller, president of the *Shaved Heads Are Sexy Club*, was so overcome with admiration that she used a picture of the wax mannequin for their Christmas card. Below his likeness she wrote, "Merry Yuletide Greetings."

Louis Armstrong loved to relate a baldheaded incident that occurred when he visited Brynner on a Hollywood movie set. "The two of us go back a long time," the famous jazz musician said. "So I stopped to say hello."

Several years before, Yul had proposed the black entertainer for membership into a club he belonged to. When Armstrong was rejected because of his color, Brynner sent the president a curt but significant note: "I quit your lilywhite organization and I'll tell my friends to do the same. In the meantime you can all go to hell."

Armstrong was gratified by his friend's prompt action. "That cat is his own man," he said. "I thought nobody could make him do something he didn't want to. But someone did—at least for a short time. In that movie they made him wear a wig.

"When it came time for the meal break he was still wearing it. I was about to start eating when all of a sudden he says, 'Satchmo, let's trade instruments—we had brought them along with us. He grabs my horn and starts blowing real hard. I start strumming his guitar. We get so carried away that someone yells for us to pipe down. So what does Yul do? He's about to toss the wig at the guy who is complaining, but he suddenly changes his mind and shoves it on the bell of my horn. Then he says, 'Admit it, Satchmo, that wig looks better on your horn than it does on me.'

"That cat may be bald on his top, but he sure has got a lot of hair on his chest."

Few scientific studies indicate that baldness produces machismo. However, four doctors from the Royal Infirmary in Bristol, England, presented their findings in a medical journal after conducting a lengthy study of alopecia (baldness) and masculinity. They concluded: "The suggestion that bald men are more virile than well-thatched contemporaries is probably an old wives' tale."

When told about the British study, Yul responded in his usual fashion by reciting a slightly vulgar gypsy proverb: "When buying a stallion, disregard the appearance up front."

Brynner claimed that he had dozens of imitators. But he was unperturbed. "The sincerest form of flattery," he said. "I can't help it if everybody wants to be just like me. All my life people have tried to copy me. I'd be dressed in black. Suddenly, it became the most fashionable men's color. I'd wear a gold chain around my neck. Every actor in Hollywood rushed out to buy one. I'd keep my shirt unbuttoned to the waist. Soon everyone's navel was showing. Now, count the baldies!"

A theater in Los Angeles conducted a "Yul Brynner Look-Alike Contest" to ballyhoo one of his movies. They announced that admission would be free to all baldheaded men and that the winner would receive a fifty-dollar prize. No one had recognized Brynner when he slipped in. He wasn't declared the winner, not even a runner-up. "Now there are people who look more like me than I do," he said.

Adlai Stevenson, another almost-bald celebrity, once asked Brynner for advice about his rapidly disappearing hairline. Yul told the Democratic candidate for president, "Adlai, get rid of the fringes. Erase the dividing line. Then no one will know whether you are a genuine egghead or not. Besides, completely bald men are more sensual!"

– CHAPTER TEN –

Home
Sweet
Homer

BRYNNER once said that he'd like to have inscribed on his tombstone: "Here lies a man who adored children of all varieties."

"He truly felt that way," said actress Mia Farrow, a close family friend. When she brought a Vietnamese orphan into her home, she named Yul the godfather. He and his wife, Jacqueline, were so impressed that they decided to do the same thing.

"It was a very wise thing to do," Brynner said. He flew to Saigon to bring back his new daughter. She was promptly named Mia. "I would never have thought that at my age I could become so consumed with love for a baby," Yul said. "Once when she was very tiny we had to leave her with a governess to fly to Hollywood. But before we could finish our business we flew back to be with Mia. Even a few days away from her was too much. If anybody had told me that just a short time ago, I would have suggested that he should examine his fool head.

"The way I felt reminded me of something Charlie Chaplain had told me on his seventieth birthday. We were sitting in his garden when he said, 'Yul, I'm a little ashamed to speak of the surprise I received when I woke up this morning. Oona told me that I was about to be a father again.' "

A short time later the Brynners decided to adopt another Vietnamese infant. She was being airlifted to the United States when her plane crashed, killing 190 other orphans. "Until we were certain of her fate," Yul said, "Jacqueline and I were nervous wrecks. For four days we wondered if she was dead, too. Fortunately, she survived. Except for a minor ear problem, the crash left no marks. We named her Melody."

When the surviving children landed in San Francisco, they were stranded. The agency that had arranged for the adoptions had run out of money to fly them to their final destinations. Yul appealed to Hugh Hefner, the publisher of *Playboy*, for help. Hefner donated his private DC-9 jet, "The Big Bunny." It ferried the children to their new homes. The bawdy magazine's bunnies acted as nursemaids.

Brynner was asked about the morality of calling upon Hefner for assistance. Yul stared at the man who had dared to inquire. "If you ask me any more of those fool questions," he said, "I'll bust you in the mouth! And I guarantee that the bust won't be of the *Playboy* variety!"

In the winter of 1974, Brynner decided to abandon his movie career and return to the legitimate theater. "I had enough of Hollywood's chicanery," he said. "Jacqueline and I wanted to live a normal life." He agreed to star in a musical comedy that was loosely based on Homer's *Odyssey*. Yul was certain it would have the same appeal that *The King and I* had had twenty-three years before.

He felt that his new play couldn't miss. The author was Eric Segal, who had written *Love Story*, a best-selling book, and the music was by Mitch Leigh, the composer of the music for *Man of La Mancha*. Brynner was to portray the wandering

Odysseus who after twenty years comes home to his still-beautiful and much-sought-after wife Penelope.

Before opening on Broadway the *Odysseus* company planned a year-long tour of Cleveland, Toronto, Detroit, Chicago, Los Angeles, San Francisco, Washington, D.C., and Boston. "I demanded an extensive tryout period," Brynner said. "I always felt that the original version of *The King and I* opened on Broadway much too soon. Once you open there and are a hit, a show tends to congeal. I wasn't going to take any chances."

As soon as his terms were agreed to, he sent out an "accommodation list" to the managers of prospective hotels he planned to stay in. Donald MacEwen, who was in charge of a small but luxurious San Francisco inn, received one. "I kept it," he said. "In all my years in the lodging business I've never seen one remotely resembling that list. I've worked in deluxe hotels all over the world—ones that catered to discriminating and demanding clienteles. King Farouk, Charles DeGaulle, Winston Churchill, Richard Nixon were among my guests. But in all that time I've never encountered greater or more imperial requests than those made by Mr. Brynner. The mere mention of his name makes me so nervous I start to itch."

MacEwen had experienced Brynner's demands before. Once when he was the manager of a large New York hotel, his staff had strict orders never to disturb him during the night unless there was an emergency of mammoth proportions. One Sunday at 3 A.M. he received an agitated phone call. "It's . . . Mr. Brynner . . ." an assistant sputtered. "He ordered blini layered with black caviar and two bottles of his special brand of wine. Somehow I was able to cope with the blini command, but there aren't any bottles of wine left. What shall we do?"

MacEwen managed to wake up the owner of a liquor

store. "It wasn't easy," he said, starting to scratch. "Nothing with Mr. Brynner ever was. Although his bill was always enormous and his checks always cleared—he was one guest I'd gladly have given to the Waldorf!"

Yul's "accommodation list," which has since become a collector's item, contained several dozen musts:

YB's suite must have large living room, kitchen, two bedrooms—one bigger than the other.

King-size bed in master bedroom. *One mattress, not two!*

Must be utterly blacked out so as not a sliver of light can enter. Though must be able to open when wanted.

Check drawer, closet and shelf space. Need plenty of all.

A gross of wooden hangers in master bedroom. Extras in all other rooms of YB's party.

Suite must be immaculate.

Accommodations cannot be on or within one floor of conventions.

YB's secretary must be on same floor. She should have large suite with kitchen. Double bed, a good size desk a must.

An electric typewriter.

YB's Yorkshire terrier will be joining us. Proper accommodations.

Outside PRIVATE telephone lines; one in living room of YB's suite.

One in second bedroom of his suite. Not an extension.

One in secretary's room.

All phones must be Touch Tone type with 13-foot cords.

Kitchen in YB's suite must have set of dishes with at least six of everything, including salad dishes, soup dishes, cups, saucers, silverware. Plus additional wine and water glasses.

All hotel managers to supply list of nearest grocery store.

A homeopathic drugstore if one in the area.

Best local throat specialist and best orthopedic doctor in the area.

Separate car available for Mrs. Brynner and secretary. Driver to be paid on hourly rate.

Wine—Chateau Larose '66. If hotel doesn't have it in its wine cellar, order in advance. One case at least per week with more available if needed.

Stock YB's kitchen in advance of his arrival with:

Two heads of Bibb lettuce. Nice, fresh.

One pound salted butter.

Jar of marinated herring in cream.

Dozen bottles of dark Heineken beer.

One pint of heavy cream.

One bottle of wine vinegar.

One box of shallots. Or if not boxed, enough for a week.

One box of special K cereal.

One box of Heartland cereal—plain.

One dozen BROWN eggs. *Under no circumstances white ones!*

Yul had a fetish about brown eggs. He claimed that the head chef at the Hotel Ritz in Paris had told him that they were superior. A Washington, D.C, reporter learned about the actor's egg idiosyncrasy and wrote a feature about it. An uproar followed. Dieticians and gourmets said that Brynner was all wrong—that there wasn't any difference. Yul wasn't accustomed to retracting statements he'd made. However, when the nation's farmers and housewives joined the protest, he issued an apology. "Maybe I erred," he said. "There's egg all over my face. But I hope they are brown ones!"

Trouble struck during *Odysseus*'s premiere in Cleveland.

"There was a newspaper strike," Yul recalled. "And it's impossible to survive without reviews. As soon as it was settled, another blow fell. I lost my voice. I could hardly speak, let alone sing. Three doctors were consulted. They all said that I had a serious throat ailment and would have to withdraw from the show."

Brynner always prided himself on having a very acute sense of responsibility toward a play he was associated with. "The thought of my infirmity being the cause of the closing and throwing all those people out of work was absolutely intolerable to me," he said. "That's when I decided upon acupuncture. You must remember that I was brought up in China, where people are more familiar with that form of treatment than they are with aspirin."

A friend of his told him about Norbu Chen, a skilled practitioner who was living in Houston. Yul chartered a plane and flew there during a heavy storm. When he arrived he had completely lost his voice.

"But an explanation wasn't necessary," he said. "Right off, Chen knew exactly what was wrong. He told me to remove my shirt and socks. Then he placed his needles at strategic points. About an hour later I was completely cured—my voice had come back."

But his prompt return to *Odysseus* didn't make much of a difference—it appeared to be doomed. Severe editing didn't help. It was too long and filled with heavy-handed lines. Brynner recoiled when he had to say, "Home is where you unpack the luggage of your soul, dirty laundry and all." He had earned a reputation of milking a line for all it was worth, but now he seemed to be waiting for the show to end.

Midway through the tour, Segal and Leigh weren't speaking to each other. Matters weren't helped when Yul lectured a congressman from Mississippi who visited him backstage. "You're a bloody hypocrite," Brynner shouted.

"You claim that you want to save the country, but you spend your time castigating blacks!"

Brynner was so riled from this encounter that he forgot the lines of his main song, *I'm Going Home Sweet Homer*. He had to deliver it in pantomime.

An editorial in a southern newspaper condemned Yul's "shocking manners" and said that he should have suffered his memory loss about a half hour earlier. Later in the week he was again in the news. Joan Diener, who played his wife, Penelope, noticed that she hadn't received her agreed-upon co-billing on the marquee. Since there wasn't time to alter it before the first act, the manager draped the entire marquee with a black cloth, leading a radio disc jockey to announce that Brynner was dead.

"I almost wished it were true," Yul said. "It was a real low point for me. I had desperately wanted another hit, but I realized that it wasn't about to happen."

During much of the tour the play received dismal notices. Critics, however, seemed reluctant to attack Yul personally. Typical was the comment in a Chicago newspaper: "Brynner is excellent but the show is from hunger."

"As soon as he was offstage he'd reach for his camera and start snapping pictures," said Rose Eldred, a wardrobe assistant. "It was his way of letting off steam. Nothing was sacred. You would pick your nose and suddenly there'd be a click. He and his camera seemed to be everywhere. A museum in one of the cities we played in set up an exhibition of some of the pictures he'd taken. Many of them were shots of young children he'd seen in a foundling home. He frequently went there, but refused to discuss it. When one nosy reporter asked him about the foundling home, Yul winked. Then he said, 'The reason I go there is because I feel that a devoted father should see his misbegotten offspring. There are thirty-five children there. All fathered by me!' The reporter knew when he was being ridiculed and walked away."

The hours Brynner wasn't in the theater or out with his camera, he could be found at home playing with his two Vietnamese daughters.

The four Brynners eventually arrived in New York with *Odysseus*, which had been renamed *Home Sweet Homer*. The gesture was a last-minute effort to try and save the play, but it failed to help. *Home Sweet Homer* opened and closed on the same night. An editor of *Variety* who had seen Brynner's hotel list commented, "Undoubtedly, it would have made a better play than this one."

When the show fizzled, Yul and his family left for Normandy. Before boarding the plane, he told reporters, "I'll be back on Broadway very soon. And when I do you'll have lots nicer things to say." He was prophetic. No sooner had he walked through the door of their French home than a cablegram arrived from New York. Lee Gruber and Shelly Gross, two American theatrical producers, wanted him to star in a revival of *The King and I*.

CHAPTER ELEVEN

Return
of
the King

MOMENTS after Brynner reported for duty in the 1977 revival of *The King and I*, he kissed the stage floor of New York's Uris Theater and remarked to Constance Towers, his latest Mrs. Anna, "I'm glad to be back on Broadway. Here's where I belong."

A quarter of a century had elapsed since he swaggered his way into stardom opposite Gertrude Lawrence in the original production. According to available records he was now in his early sixties—he claimed to be fifty-seven. When he had first undertaken the part of King Mongkut he was in his thirties. "Much too young to play a monarch with so many wives," he said. "Since then I've learned a lot. Am I not now more knowing? Have I not become a superior actor? Do I not have more psychic energy?" he asked. In Socratic fashion he answered his own questions. "Yes!" he said, tolerating no dissent.

As soon as he agreed to repeat the role he went into strict training on his farm in Normandy. He lost twenty-seven pounds. Every morning he ran three kilometers—backwards. It was a trick he had learned from his friend Luis Miguel Dominguin, who was getting into shape for his return to the bullring after a long retirement.

"It develops a completely different set of muscles," Brynner said. "It's a marvelous exercise. But of course I built my body during my early teens. After you pass twenty it's usually too late. I started out in the circus as a trapeze artist when I was very young and I've stayed in good shape ever since."

To prove his point he challenged reporters to a push-up contest. His nearest opponent dropped out at eighteen. "For an average person that's pretty good," he said condescendingly as he continued his demonstration. He stopped at thirty-five, dismissing his wheezing with, "I forgot to take my morning glass of champagne."

He said that he hadn't slept the previous night. "But then I detest too much sleep," he told the reporters. "It's such a waste of time." He volunteered that he usually didn't shut his eyes for more than a few hours a night. "Four hours at a maximum. Sleep is purely a habit. I've had that habit since I was thirteen. It allows me to do a lot of things other people have no time for. In my forty years of professional life, the extra hours I've saved from not sleeping have added up to a tremendous number of additional things I was able to accomplish."

When one of the newspapermen mentioned that Brynner's former wife Doris's name was being closely linked to Stavros Niarchos, the Greek shipping tycoon, Yul nodded. "That proves that I can only be replaced by someone who has something outstanding about him," he said. Niarchos was reputed to be one of the wealthiest men in the world.

Toward the end of the press conference, Brynner became very angry when the play was referred to as a revival. "It's as much that as *Hamlet* is!" he shouted. He said that a revival was seldom more than a two-time proposition. It happened when a shrewd producer believed that the time was ripe to repeat a success and thus make a killing. But a play of the caliber of *The King and I* was very different. He said that over the years it had become a classic and deserved to be shown again and again.

His rage continued when a weekly newsmagazine writer asked if he identified with the king offstage. "That's a damned foolish question," Yul snapped. "It shows total ignorance on your part. Life wouldn't be livable if I came home from the theater and approached Jacqueline as the King of Siam. Only in the play have I ever identified myself with the character."

Still, his home contained a throne. When reminded of this, he bellowed, "The throne was given to me as a gag! I don't think I ever sat on the bloody thing!"

"But he did," said Irene Baker, a former Brynner maid. "I'd come in to dust and there he'd be stretched out on it. All he needed was some kind of crown to make it official. If anyone thought of himself as a true blue blood, it was Mr. Brynner. But I'll say this for him—he was a powerfully decent boss to work for. Once I told him that my daughter had multiple sclerosis and had to miss a lot of her classes. Right off he arranged for her to go to a special school. When she finished up with high honors he went to her graduation. Mr. Brynner was a good man, God rest his soul."

Harold Oberman, a Manhattan taxi driver, had the same impression. "Lots of times I'd pick him up at the theater," he recalled. "I'd say, 'Where to, King?' And his answer would be, 'To my castle.' He'd call me 'court jester.' It kept on like that for the entire trip. When it was over I could always count on a hefty tip."

During the show's fifty-week Broadway run there was rarely an empty seat—the SRO sign was frequently posted. Terrance Milgram, a traffic policeman assigned to the theater, said, "Each time he tried to reach his car, squealing ladies mobbed him. I don't think Sinatra at the top of his prime had it so good. I'd see eighty-year-old grandmothers and their sixteen-year-old granddaughters claw to get a look at him. I used to wonder what a guy with a completely bald noodle had that I didn't. I soon found out—charm. So much that he could bottle it."

Most critics felt that Yul's characterization of the autocratic Siamese monarch was more powerful than it had been before. On the stage he still paced his lavish court like a caged lion threatening to shatter his bars while ravishing the heart of every lady in the audience. But there seemed to be a new depth to his performance. Without adding lines, his gestures and behavior now clearly pointed out the cultural collision course between East and West. He listened more intently to Anna's outlandish ideas. Although he continued to be overbearing, he would be serious, a moment later puzzled, then become extremely animated. He no longer had to rely on dialogue—his body spoke for him. By the time he died in the last scene the entire audience was under his spell.

He was one of the few original performers to appear in the new version. Several of the young boys and girls who had played his children in the first show now had minor adult parts. The current play was directed by Yuriko, who had formerly been the lead in the dance scene. Her daughter, Susan, now had that role. Wisely, Yuriko gave Brynner few orders on how to act. "Just be yourself," she told him. "No one but you knows how to really play the king."

"Her words were flattering," Yul said. "She listened when I told her that the emphasis should shift slightly. I made the audience aware that Anna stood for human rights—the rights of women to function as human beings as well as men. It was the ladies in the audience who spotted this."

What had been a pleasant but rather dewy tale of the taming of a barbarian had become a graceful, tough-minded battle of the sexes, with a hero whose outsized ego was vulnerable and a heroine who wanted to be treated as a dignified, emancipated woman.

These days we're lucky to walk out of a new musical

able to whistle one happy tune. From *The King and I* you could take your pick of a dozen. Four of the songs: *Getting to Know You, Shall We Dance, Hello, Young Lovers,* and *I Whistle a Happy Tune* were played so frequently on radio and television that during one interview Yul said, "It's good to hear them instead of the trash singers belt out these days." He then proceeded to illustrate what he meant by reciting some modern lyrics. His performance was widely reported, causing Elvis Presley to make threatening noises. "The next time Ah run into him," said the rajah of rock and roll, "Ah'll kick his butt!"

"I have a small backside," Yul replied. "I suggest that he aim at a larger target." When the two met, it was very sedate—they exchanged autographs and complimented each other's performances.

Brynner rarely received any catcalls from the audience. He did, however, after he made his Presley remark. A teenager sitting in the balcony shouted, "Elvis is the real king. Not you!"

The theater manager was certain that Yul would reply. He needn't have worried. Brynner gave the heckler one of his haughtiest stares and continued being the arrogant king. A few days later a probably unrelated incident occurred. A man waving a gun charged past the doorkeeper.

"He was caught before he could do any damage," Yul said. "But after that I was told to use the back entrance coming and going. But they weren't concerned about the other members of the cast. When one of the dancers was actually mugged inside the theater and had her purse stolen, I decided things had gone far enough. I promised the cast that I'd take care of security. I've always felt that I was the captain of the ship and had to protect my crew.

"When I asked the management to provide us with the necessary guards, they refused. So I went out to the nearest boxing gym and hired them myself. Tough-looking customers. One of them was so powerful that when he leaned against the brass rail behind the last row he broke it. Another one kept breaking seats every time he sat down. Word got around that these big bruisers were patrolling the place. Overnight, we became the most secure theater in New York. After all, something had to be done to protect the cast."

Brynner enjoyed a good working relationship with most of the actors. He attended their parties, listened to their gossip, handed out advice. Ever since 1974, Yul had been warning them not to eat pork when dining out. He claimed that an order of spare ribs had given him trichinosis. He sued the offending restaurant for $3 million. When the case finally came to court, Yul was fully prepared. Dressed entirely in a black silk suit, he limped to the witness chair and assumed his famous arms-crossed-over-the-chest posture. In a grieving voice he told the five-woman, three-man jury that his wife had been deprived of his lovemaking due to the trichinosis.

"This illness has not only affected my body, but my entire life," he said. "It has plagued my career ever since that fateful day!"

He complained that because of it he still suffered severe leg cramps. "My legs ache when I have to sit for long periods," he told the judge. Several times during his testimony he was granted permission to stand. When an attorney for the defense suggested that he might not be telling the entire truth, Yul charged out of the witness chair. He had to be restrained.

The case was settled out of court for $125,000. When he was handed the check he said triumphantly, "Every man, woman, and child has a sacred obligation to fight back. To relinquish that right would bring on chaos."

Brynner never was reticent about making his views known. His friend Noël Coward once said, "Yul regards

himself as an authority on everything. And he's fully prepared to discuss his opinions at the drop of a hemline."

Newspaper editors discovered that his often-unortho-
dox opinions made excellent copy. William Wilkerson, foun-
der of *The Hollywood Reporter*, said, "Whenever I need a colorful
quote I call him up. He never fails me."

During the revival of *The King and I*, Brynner became a
frequent guest on television and radio talk shows. After delivering a few thousand words on a large variety of subjects
ranging from actors in politics to ladies' bosoms, he would
usually end his one-man conversations with a phrase he
made popular in the show: "Etcetera, etcetera, etcetera."

He was asked about the wisdom of having an actor in
the White House. In his long-winded reply he said, "Just
because you are a good actor and can play characters that
are liked, why should people vote for you? Usually actors in
general have a tendency to react on a purely emotional level
because such is the nature of our work. Actors are not capable
of taking really a studied and calculated and intellectual view
of things."

Immediately after his political lesson he launched into
a harangue about padded brassieres. "I'll undoubtedly be
called a male chauvinist when I say this. But despite the
current practice of burning bras, too many women still try
to disguise themselves in order to measure up to what they
think are popular standards of beauty. I'm sick and tired of
looking at those mountainous bosoms. The ones that are
fashioned with wire and rubber. To me, it doesn't matter if
ladies have less bosom as long as it is alive."

Then without taking a deep breath he started discussing
children. Brynner should have been on safer ground, but
here, too, his unconventional views startled his listeners.
"Mothers and fathers," he told them, "should occasionally
change places with their offspring. The children become the

parents, and parents the children. That would give all parents much clearer views of their awesome responsibilities."

Backstage he was still teacher and father-confessor to the thirteen boys and girls in the cast. Not only did he teach them acting lore, but continued to have definite opinions on nonperforming problems. Often, he combined the two. Several of the youngsters asked him how they could keep out of mischief. Before replying he consulted his friend, pediatrician Dr. Benjamin Spock.

The next day Yul bought each child in the production a drawing pad and crayons. He instructed them on how to sketch scenes from the show. He said the best ones would be prominently displayed. For the next three weeks when not needed on stage the king's children were too busy drawing to engage in any pranks. When the time came to make the selection, he gravely announced that the contest had ended in a dead heat. As a result, thirteen pictures appeared on the upper promenade of the Uris Theater. Brynner was the proud guide.

The 1977 revival enjoyed a highly successful Broadway run—ticket sales were more than $12 million. Attractive offers came from all parts of the world. A theatrical producer in Johannesburg, South Africa, guaranteed him twice the salary he received in New York plus a large percentage of the profits. Yul refused. This was long before apartheid became the subject of protests in the United States. "I won't bring the show to a country that legalizes segregation," he said.

Instead, he opened in Chicago, where for six weeks he continued to play to overflow audiences. When he was given the key to the city, he remarked that he preferred the seating arrangement in the Chicago theater to the one that would have existed in South Africa. "Here anyone of any color can sit next to you," he said. "All they need is a small fortune to be able to buy a ticket."

The children in the play were getting restless as *The King and I* neared the end of its run. "I knew that I had to do something drastic when they started tossing spitballs and tripping each other right on stage," Yul said. "And that it had to be a lot more than drawing pictures. As a rule I'm very much opposed to bribing a child. But I changed my mind when I saw how unorderly they were becoming. I promised that I'd buy each of them a present if they'd behave until the very last performance. Before agreeing they caucused. Then their spokesman spoke up. 'It's a deal,' he said, 'if you make it a *big* present!' You can see why I'm partial to working with children. They're far more honest than adults."

Early in February, the company traveled to Los Angeles to perform for ten weeks. It was their final stop. The costumes, scenery, and lighting equipment had become so elaborate that twenty-two trucks and four baggage cars were required to move them. Four seamstresses set up sewing machines backstage to keep the costumes trim. Brynner was their best customer.

When asked about this, he replied diplomatically, "Doesn't your lovely city deserve lovely costumes?" The reporters were suprised by Yul's saccharine reply. They were certain it would change after the next question. "How many actresses have you been overly friendly with?" he was asked.

"I regard everybody as my friend," he replied. The interview continued placidly until a reporter wanted to know if Yul enjoyed playing in Los Angeles. "I like L.A. fine," he said. "Once I can forget how close it is to the film capital. You know, Hollywood almost ruined my career!" It was probably the only time he overtly admitted his less than spectacular critical success as a movie actor.

In the summer of 1979, Yul flew to London to costar with Virginia McKenna at the Palladium. Before he agreed to play King Mongkut in England, he had insisted that extensive alterations be made backstage. He gave the management a list of changes he wanted. To keep him happy they knocked down a wall of the star's dressing room and combined it with a former chorus practice hall. Added were a Jacuzzi, wall-to-wall carpeting, an electrically operated massage chair, a full-size mirror in the shower, a bidet, new plumbing that provided "extra-strong" water pressure, and a complete paint job. The cost of his requests amounted to more than $50,000.

He explained the necessity of demanding an adequate dressing room. "Most theater managers are tightfisted," he said. "And that single coat of brown paint is a very frugal way to cover all the filth that accumulates on the dressing room walls. The carpeting is essential because most of the cast of *The King and I* perform barefoot. Some people think the full-size mirror in the shower is an affect, but I need it to examine myself carefully. I play the role so vigorously that I constantly get bruises and scratches. As for the rest, I must have comfort backstage because that is where I spend half of my time. Two hours to get ready, three hours on stage, two to get my makeup off and unwind. I have to have some joy backstage if I'm expected to spread joy in the front."

Satisfied with his new dressing room, he rented a furnished apartment in fashionable Belgravia for $2300 a week, and a chauffeured Rolls Royce on twenty-four-hour call for $1150 a week. For the four months that Yul appeared at the Palladium he regularly brought the audience to its feet. His old friend Rex Harrison said, "I was so awed by him that I lost my voice shouting 'Bravo.' "

Lord Louis Mountbatten, uncle of Prince Philip and last Viceroy of India, saw the show three times. "No one can ever rival Brynner's performance," he said. To convey his pleasure he took Yul on a personally conducted tour of central London. Most of the traveling was done on the city's famous double-decker buses. Among the stops were Buckingham Palace, Westminister Abbey, Parliament, and Number 10 Downing Street.

While dining on fish and chips on Hyde Park Corner, Brynner serenaded his host with several of the songs from the show. Mountbatten begged Yul to teach him the words. He then joined the actor in a duet. The following day Yul received a thank-you note from his grateful royal partner. It was enclosed in a toy London bus.

During the Palladium stand, Brynner became aware of four-foot-nine-inch, twenty-one-year-old Kathy Lee, one of the dancers in the Eliza number. "Although she had a small part she stood out," he recalled. "She had that rare combination of beauty, grace, and ability." He made inquiries about her.

Kathy, who was born in Malaysia, began studying ballet when she was a very young child. In her teens she was taken to England to continue her dancing at the London Royal Academy. She graduated at the top of her class. Her teachers predicted that she would have an outstanding classical career.

"I so wanted to be a purist," Kathy said. "But I also wanted to eat and there wasn't any demand for that kind of dancing. One day I picked up a trade paper and saw an audition notice for *The King and I*. At the time I didn't have the slightest knowledge of Siamese dancing. However, I tried out and was hired."

When Yul met Kathy he was still wed to Jacqueline, but that didn't stop him from vigorously courting the young dancer. "He was really smitten," said Jean Levin. "He wouldn't stop talking about her. How she would become the world's foremost ballerina. How she was the loveliest woman he'd ever met."

As soon as the show closed, Yul retired to his farm in Normandy but commuted regularly to the United States. He and Kathy were frequently seen together. When reporters asked him about his marital status, he snapped, "My private life is no concern of yours!"

Despite long-term efforts by gifted gossip reporters to get Yul to discuss the breakup of his marriage, he refused to talk about it. All he would tell them was that he and Jacqueline were drifting in opposite directions. "Unfortunately," he said, "that happens to the most devoted husband and wife. I guess that even applies to me."

Prudent investments and tremendous acting salaries had made him a very wealthy man. "I don't have to work any more," he said. "I can stay home, drink champagne by the case, and eat caviar by the pound." On one of his trips to New York, he was given an autographed copy of a book his son had recently written, *The Ballad of Habit and Accident*. Although Rock called it a novel, critics thought it to be a not-so-thinly-disguised autobiography. Yul wasn't presented as the most enlightened parent, yet he raised no howl about any of the negative passages. Instead, he spoke glowingly of his son's literary ability.

During his "inactive period," as he called it, Brynner accepted the honorary presidency of the Second Romany Congress, which was held in Geneva. At the conclusion of the four-day meeting he told the representatives from twenty-two nations they were looking at a man who owed all his success to his gypsy heritage. He delivered an impassioned speech about how gypsies had been segregated in ghettos and concentration camps during World War II. "The Nazis used us as slave labor," he said. "When we were too weak to work they resorted to murder. They killed 50,000 of our brothers and sisters." He ended his talk in Romany: *"Baktalo amor drom"* (From now on may our road be a lucky one).

He continued to do volunteer work for many worthy causes: the United Nations, the Red Cross, the NAACP, the Salvation Army, various health organizations, the March of Dimes, French and Swiss youth groups; he wrote frequent letters to the editor condemning ultraconservative practices; he coauthored a cookbook that featured recipes "Fit for a

King." The *Library Journal* called it "better than usual celebrity cookbooks." But Yul wasn't happy being a man of leisure. Little coaxing was necessary to convince him to appear in yet another revival of *The King and I.*

On February 18, 1981, Brynner opened in Washington, D.C. He had signed a contract with Mitch Leigh to make a coast-to-coast tour that would eventually wind up on Broadway. That incredible, heroic journey will go down as one of the most poignant chapters in show business history.

"In all the years I've been connected with the theater," said Robert Lantz, Yul's longtime agent, "I've never witnessed anything comparable."

CHAPTER TWELVE

The Farewell Tour

"IN the minds of millions of people," said television interviewer Barbara Walters, "Yul Brynner and *The King and I* are as firmly coupled as the Statue of Liberty and the United States."

When Yul heard about it he said, "I guess the reason Barbara compared the two of us was that she felt we both badly needed repairs." He was referring to the Statue's recent overhaul and the treatment he had received for lung cancer. The disease was diagnosed late in September of 1983. He tried to keep it secret, but the news leaked out.

One of the songs King Mongkut sings is about trying to live another day, to do his best for one more day. These lines were always greeted with bursts of frenzied applause, interrupting the song. Cancer didn't mellow him; he would glower at the offenders.

It was in Los Angeles that Yul learned about his malignancy. Kathy, whom he had recently married, had made an appointment with an internist for a checkup for herself. He asked if he might go along. "I've noticed this tiny lump on my neck," he said. "I guess it should be looked at."

Dr. Paul Rednick, Kathy's doctor, examined the actor and ordered an immediate biopsy. Brynner, who admitted to having smoked five packs of cigarettes a day, had cancer. X-rays revealed that tumors were present in each lung and that the cancer had spread to his lymph system. Kathy insisted on a second and third and fourth medical opinion. All of them were exactly the same: an advanced case of cancer. An operation was impossible. It was suggested that radiation might slow the cancer down.

"When I first found out," Brynner said, "I didn't want to try anything. I kept thinking, Why did it happen to me? Kathy and I had only been married a very short while. Had I been fair to her? Nothing seemed worthwhile. All I could think about was something I had learned from the gypsies: *You are born alone, you live alone, and you die alone.*

"Suddenly, I realized the saying wasn't completely accurate. I decided to fight back—to lick the illness. I credit Kathy with giving me the will. She now was the lead dancer in the show, but somehow she devoted her full energy to me. Without her constant support I'd have caved in."

Six times a week, before going to the theater, Brynner visited Los Angeles' Cedars Sinai Medical Center for a two-hour-long radiation treatment. "I went there for eight weeks," he said. "During all that time I didn't miss a performance."

Throughout that period Yul refused to discuss his condition with other members of the cast. "It wasn't that he was being aloof," Kathy said. " 'Why make them uncomfortable?' he'd say. I could see that he was in great pain, but he rarely complained. The radiation had badly burned his bronchial tube, making it almost impossible for him to swallow. A good part of the time he'd be so sick at his stomach that he couldn't eat. Again, he didn't complain. He wanted us to live as near normal a life as possible. I think at times I was the one with the long face. Never once did he refer to it as cancer. Only the illness."

Despite the gloomy medical report, he was now more optimistic. He kept telling his physicians that they would become famous when the public learned that they had cured Yul Brynner. "Once he joked about Halley's Comet," a doctor recalled. "He told me that not only did he intend to see it in 1986 but also when it returned in 2062. It was pretty obvious that he was hurting, but he refused to bellyache. Instead, he kidded around and carried on with the show."

While undergoing the radiation treatment, Yul met a ten-year-old boy who had also been diagnosed as having cancer. The youngster refused to cooperate with his doctors. "What's the use?" was his attitude.

"Mr. Brynner provided him with positive answers," said one of the nurses. "He took that kid under his wing and made him see that life was worth fighting for. Those two were constantly in close huddle. One time Mr. Brynner invited him to a matinee of *The King and I*. Until then I don't think the boy realized how big a star Mr. Brynner really was. As soon as he found out he said to me, 'When I grow up I'm going on the stage just like him.' "

On Thanksgiving Day the show ended its Los Angeles run. The Brynners had heard about an immunologist in Hanover, West Germany, who claimed success with cancer victims by treating them with special diets and herbal injections. Although the unorthodox program was frowned on by most American physicians, Yul decided to try it. For the two weeks he was a patient at the Hanover clinic he consumed massive doses of vitamins, minerals, and plant extracts. "Right away, I felt I was improving," Brynner said. "It continued. I started gaining weight and began feeling like my old self. The treatment had worked."

When Kathy felt that her husband was fit to travel they flew to New York, where he underwent a series of tests. At the conclusion Yul was told that he was in remission. "Those doctors are being too conservative," he said. "I'm in *permanent* remission. I've licked the Big C."

A few days later he resumed the tour in Baltimore.

Reviewers wrote that he was still the undisputed King of Siam. After three weeks of playing to a packed house, he and *The King and I* company moved on to other major cities: Kansas City, Cincinnati, St. Louis, Vancouver, Portland, Milwaukee, Toronto, Boston, Cleveland, Chicago, Washington, D.C.

In most of them he visited hospitals where he encouraged cancer patients with stories of his own remarkable recovery. "I decided it was better to be on the stage in front of 2,000 people than at home self-pitying in a sickbed," he'd tell them. "You're thinking that the choice only applies to me. Well, you're wrong. You all have comparable options. I survived and so can you!"

Upon completing the out-of-town tour, Yul took *The King and I* to New York, where he and Kathy bought a three-bedroom co-op apartment near the United Nations. "We intend to make it our second home," he said. "Next to Normandy, New York is the best place to live."

Once again critics had kind words for his performance, but it was obvious that their reviews were tempered by sentiment. Yul's latest effort was called, "Memorable . . . One doesn't go to see the show for any fresh interpretive angles. One goes to bow."

Brynner was only partly pleased with the comments. He said, "It's true that I've played the role for a long time, but almost every day I keep adding new insights. And my recent bout with illness hasn't changed that." He maintained that he had little trouble in keeping the king fresh. "He changes all the time as we do in life," Yul said. "I could never play him mechanically—I wouldn't know how to go on stage that way. Each performance has to be a whole new experience. Sometimes, Mary Beth Piel, my new Anna, doesn't know what to expect from me.

"I can't even fully explain it myself. It's something that happens while I'm making myself up and I'm alone. Then I like to sit on stage left, where the stage manager sits during the overture. I get the audience's pulse from their reaction to the music, from their sound. It doesn't even consciously enter my mind. It's instinctive. It's spontaneous. Are they sluggish and slow? Are they open and eager? You must develop a sense that you're a storyteller and you're presenting the story for the first time to this peculiar bunch of living people. The greatest miscalculation an actor can make is to take the audience for granted. I've preached this rationale over and over."

Some of Brynner's colleagues may have been intimidated by him, but they respected him because of his outspoken views. More than a hundred of them toasted him at Le Dome, an elegant New York restaurant. "It's not uncommon for showbiz folks to honor one of their own," said Carol Channing. "People get up and mouth niceties they don't really mean. But in this case it was very different. Everyone was there to pay tribute to an extraordinary man."

William Hammerstein, Oscar's son, was master of ceremonies. He started the festivities by saying, "Yul got his crown the old-fashioned way—he earned it." Then he presented him with a silver champagne bucket that was engraved: "Every day I do my best for one more day."

"I'm delighted to accept it," Brynner said. "Except that I do it eight times a week."

Many of the guests continued to pay Yul glowing tributes. He seemed happiest when Carol Channing referred to him as "the greatest musical comedy star to come out of Outer Mongolia."

Mary Martin got the group to sing along as she circulated around the tables serenading the guests with a chorus of *Getting to Know You*. When she reached Yul, he grabbed her and pretended to be irritated. Gruffly he remarked, "If not for your persistent interference, I'd be comfortably back in television holding down a high-paying directing job!" Then he kissed her and added, "Thank you, Mary, for being such a blessed busybody!"

Yul was pleased when a newspaper called *The King and I* "a three-generation classic." He felt the description was very accurate. "Middle-aged men and women tell me that their parents had seen the original 1951 production," he said. "They saw the revival in the late 1970s, and their children saw it ten years later. I suppose it should make me feel old, but instead it makes me feel exhilarated.

"There are damned few attractions you can safely take a child to see. Many of them should have X ratings. But this has always been a clean show. Yet, it covers so very much ground. The confrontations are immortal. Man and woman, East and West, human rights, age gap, and the necessity of showing respect. If the world is allowed to continue, it will be played for centuries."

Although the play and the actor had grown old together, Yul had never given much thought to age. "I figured it was for other people," he said. "Not me. It just never occurred to me that one day I'd look in the mirror and discover wrinkles. I suppose I thought of myself as Mary Martin's Peter Pan—forever young."

During the Broadway run he was visited by many dignitaries who kept telling him how courageous he was. One of the most impassioned callers was Queen Sirikit of Thailand. Her visit was memorable because the show had been banned in her country on the grounds that it portrayed the king as a socially inadequate barbarian who had to be taught simple table manners. All was forgotten when the queen, accompanied by five ladies-in-waiting, was escorted backstage to meet Brynner. She thanked him "for a wonderful evening that was provided by the possessor of undaunted lion-heartedness."

As Queen Sirikit was about to leave, she noticed several photographs tacked to his dressing room wall. She inquired about them. They were pictures he'd taken of his four children. Soon, Yul and the queen were discussing their respective offspring. Proudly, he told her that Rock, who was nearing forty, was the manager of a society café and finishing a new novel. Twenty-four-year-old Victoria lived in Paris, where she was France's most popular model. And his younger daughters, fourteen-year-old Mia and thirteen-year-old Melody, were the prettiest and most talented teenagers he'd ever met.

The revival was due to end its run in May, but it was extended to June thirtieth. Toward the final weeks it was very evident that he was suffering severely. Questioned about his condition, he claimed it was due to a recurring back problem that was a carryover from his circus fall. On several occasions an announcement preceded the first act: "Mr. Brynner has a serious throat and ear infection."

During June he missed seven performances. When he did appear his solo song, *A Puzzlement*, was omitted. The *Shall We Dance?* number, which required him to whirl around the stage, was slowed down considerably. Often it looked as if Mary Beth Piel was carrying him around. Still, his monarchical stomping and posturing, his scowl, his burning eyes continued to dominate the show.

The box office ticket price for the last week was raised. The top price for orchestra seats was now seventy-five dollars, up from forty-five dollars. Yul was told that the sales had amounted to $533,248, an all-time weekly high.

"Why shouldn't they come to see me one more time?" he asked. But it was obvious that his fans' loyalty pleased him.

At 9:40 P.M. on June thirtieth, as the final curtain came down, the audience rose to its feet and started singing *Auld Lang Syne*. It reached a crescendo when Yul came out to bow. He stood motionless, staring at the audience for several seconds. Then he walked over to Kathy, who had played the lead royal dancer. He led her up the back steps of the set. At the top they waved and very slowly disappeared in the wings of the Broadway Theater.

Brynner had never regarded himself as a particularly sentimental person, but members of the cast said that he had to restrain himself from crying when he looked at all the tear-stricken faces. He was asked if this was really his last farewell performance. Speaking very hoarsely, he said, "I want to satisfy my need for a good quality of life that is no longer supplied by the show. Friends, concerts, and art will get more attention in an effort to renew myself." He left himself an out when he added, "There is always the possibility that someday in the future I may be required to give a command performance. How can I refuse?"

The day after the play closed the Brynners flew to France. After spending a very subdued month in Normandy, they returned to New York. "He wanted to be near Broadway," Kathy said. "He knew he was very ill, but refused to reveal how serious his condition really was. 'Why upset my friends?' he continued to say."

"But I think the reason behind it," said one of them, "was that he wanted us to remember him as the strong and dynamic person he had been throughout his life. Even at the very end Kathy shaved his head. He was that proud—wanted to die bald—his theatrical signature!"

On September fourth, two months after the final curtain of *The King and I*, an ambulance brought him to New York Hospital. His admittance was treated like a top military secret. He was listed as Robby Lee from Norwalk, Connecticut, and the entire staff was warned that to reveal any information about him would result in instant dismissal. Despite the subterfuge, reporters learned of the hospitalization. They were told that Brynner was suffering from a mild case of bacterial meningitis. However, few outsiders were permitted to see him.

A chaplain attached to the hospital asked Brynner about his faith and belief. "Yes, I am a man of faith," Yul replied. "I believe in a higher organization. You can call it God. You can call it Allah. You can call it Mohammed. You can call it anything you want. But I believe. Yes, absolutely."

Two weeks later, he lapsed into a coma from which he never recovered.

Kathy was given a small room next to his, but seldom used it. "She was at his side constantly," a nurse said. "It was almost as if she felt that somehow she could breathe life into him. But I'm sure she knew his hours were numbered."

On Thursday, October 10, 1985, Brynner died. Kathy and his four children were at his bedside. That night, marquee lights along Broadway were dimmed, dozens of theatergoers wore black bands on their sleeves, radio and television stations broadcast interviews with his friends. Mary Martin, who had discovered him, said, "The King is dead, but his portrayal of the Siamese monarch will live on for a long, long time."

A statement was issued by Josh Ellis, the actor's press representative: "He faced death with a dignity and strength that astonished his doctors." He could have added one of Yul's favorite gypsy proverbs: *Hold off buying the coffin until the corpse is laid out on the table.*

Four months after his death, Kathy and some of Yul's friends conducted a memorial service in New York City. It was held at the Shubert Theater. Hundreds of mourners strung out along West Forty-fourth Street waiting for admission. They were of all ages. Ralph Urso, who manages a video store in Boston, waited for more than three hours. "It's out of respect that I've come all this way," he said. "I so admired the guy. His movie cassettes have become some of our hottest items. Not just old or middle-aged people check them out. Teenagers also ask for them. Suddenly, he has become a cult figure—even more than Bogart or Wayne."

Carole Silverman, former president of the Philadelphia chapter of the Brynner fan club, also waited patiently in line. She wiped her tears as she said, "Sure, he had his faults. But despite them or because of them, he was outstanding. You could always count on him to make his audience feel they were mingling with aristocracy. What a wonderful, unbelievable movie his life story would make. Too bad he can't star in it."

Mike Wallace, one of the speakers at the service, said, "He was born with an extra quart of champagne in his blood—and knew how to pass it around."

But even after death, Yul continues to pass it around. Recently, the American Cancer Society began using a thirty-second commercial that was made shortly before he died of lung cancer. "Now that I'm gone," Yul says, "I tell you, don't smoke!" While delivering the chilling message, the artificially baldheaded, imperious-looking actor seems to be thinking: "Naturally, you'll do as I say! Am I not the King?"

− CHAPTER THIRTEEN −

Was Yul's Career Wasted?

FOR most of his life, Brynner succeeded in presenting himself as a mysterious person from almost nowhere. Like Topsy, the black slave child in *Uncle Tom's Cabin*, his credo seemed to be, "Nobody raised me. I just growed." The actor with the aggressively shaved head offered little accurate information about his parents, childhood, upbringing, education, ethnic and class origin. Even when he promised to reveal intimate background details, they were vague or remote or mocking. Over the years, he seemed to have forgotten how to distinguish fact from fantasy.

Unlike many of his stage and screen cohorts, Yul had little use for psychoanalysis. "The day anyone stretches me out on a couch," he used to say, "I'll be either drunk or dead." Nevertheless, several professional people who deal with human personality have been fascinated by him and had an informal go at long-distance analysis based on his known behavior. The panel consisted of Dr. Charles Goldman, a psychiatrist from Columbia, S.C.; Dr. Joyce Wike, Professor Emeritus of Nebraska Wesleyan University's Department of Sociology; Dr. Myra Nicholson, a Newark, New Jersey clinical psychologist. Here are some of their observances:

Brynner may have told so many extravagant tales about his early life because he felt the real thing was too pedestrian. He wasn't satisfied that his father was a conventional businessman or his mother an ordinary housewife. And when he realized that his farfetched stories drew attention, he continued to dramatize his past until he, too, believed the fabrications.

With little formal education, he was sort of a chameleon who could quickly absorb the culture of any place he came to rest. When he spoke, you had the impression that he was well bred, well educated, well informed, and well connected. Yet, he was convinced that to be presentable required a long string of academic degrees—which he invented. His conversations usually revolved around "I," but he studded them with big first names: "Pablo and I . . ."

When he was a very young child he started believing that courageous nonconformists got major slices of the pie. He decided that he, too, would be unconventional. What better way than to purposely shear off all his hair? Western culture associated baldness with being fat and old. Here was a young, lean, muscular man without hair. Instantly, it made him stand out and appear to be invincible.

Although his bald head became his trademark, he strenuously objected to having anyone associate it with his prominence. He was reluctant to share credit with anybody—or anything.

He liked to think that his outrageous behavior was merely a nose-thumbing gesture that could be turned off at any time he chose. Perhaps it was so in the early days, but as the years rolled on, it became more and more a part of his personality.

Actually, he was a bit of a con man. He had loads of personal charm and turned it on instinctively and guilelessly. So much so that he not only got people to do what he wanted, but he made them want to do it. He was able to exploit and manipulate others without feeling guilt.

He was quite emotional but learned to play it cool for the most part, reserving temper and passion for the moments he felt it would score. Then the explosion was impressive, memorable, and effective. He tended to be unduly optimistic or pessimistic in spite of actual facts. "Everything will turn out all right" or "The sky is falling and I'm underneath it."

It appears that Yul suffered from asthma. This respiratory disease may have a psychogenic component, and could be a manifestation of stifled emotions and unshed tears.

His insistence on being identified with gypsies and always quoting them was probably due to the romantic image he felt they portrayed. More importantly, no other actor claimed such a heritage. It allowed him to be unique.

In his dealings with his intimates, he could be deceptive to the point of being sly and even ruthless—although he would hotly deny it. On the other hand, his relationship with fellow actors, children, and members of minority groups seemed to be sincere, unqualified, and without opportunism.

He rarely admitted that he was in the wrong; therefore, there wasn't any need to apologize for anything. Even some of the perfectly dreadful movies he made, which another artist would have found humiliating, were justified with a laugh and, "Look at the box office!"

There was a paradox in his vehement belief that wealth does not produce creativeness, then his turning around to pursue a second-rate film career that guaranteed him large monetary rewards. But here, too, his philosophy seemed to be: "It applies to the other guy, not to me."

People had deep affectionate feelings about him, enjoyed and defended him. He expected it unconditionally, no matter how he trespassed on their rights. He demanded and received constant attention and admiration. However, he found it difficult to accept adulation without resorting to witticism.

He hotly denied being influenced by his role of king, yet he relished playing the part in real life. His rationalization was that his court demanded it—why disappoint them?

Not only did he believe that real men succeeded at whatever they tried, but they also had to possess excessive strength. Aware of his own physical ability, Brynner constantly issued challenges. It wasn't dissimilar from his need to appeal to every woman. His coat of arms might have contained the words: "I can best everyone in the house!"

Remember the myth of Narcissus, who fell in love with his own image in the water? Well, Brynner had little doubt that he, too, was a man of stellar destiny. Only his deeds, his thoughts, his body mattered—everything else was superfluous or a tribute to him. He was convinced of his superiority— with good reason. He was superior. But it was his own assailable belief in his uniqueness, talent, and graces that is the key to understanding him.

Was his career wasted? Yes, to some extent. He was crushed by cash-blind Hollywood producers and betrayed by his own avariciousness. He claimed that he could have effectively played Richard III, King Lear, Ahab, Shaw's Caesar, but he never gave himself the chance to find out. Perhaps he was afraid to or felt that it wasn't necessary to indulge his adoring fans. Early on he realized they liked him just as he was—*a primo macho bastard with a heart of gold!*

Play Chronology

TWELFTH NIGHT by William Shakespeare

Opened December 8, 1941, at New York's Little Theater
Cast (in order of appearance):

Beatrice Straight	Viola
Frank Rader	Sea Captain
Ronald Bennett	Sebastian
Charles Barnett	2nd Sea Captain
John Flynn	Orsino
Nelson Harrell	Curio
Lester Bacharach	Valentine
Ford Rainey	Sir Toby Belch
Mary Haynsworth	Maria
Hurd Hatfield	Sir Andrew Ague-cheek
Alan Harkness	Feste
Sam Schatz	Malvolio
Mary Lou Taylor	Olivia
Youl Bryner	Fabian

Directors: Michael Chekhov, George Shadnoff; music: Joseph Wood, Jr.; technical adviser: Johannes Larsen; presented by the Chekhov Theater Players.

L'ANNONCE FAITE À MARIE by Paul Claudel

Benefit performance given May 20, 1942, at the Barbizon Plaza Theater
Cast:

Ludmilla Pitoeff	Violaine
Youl Bryner	Pierre de Craon
Varvara Pitoeff	Mara
Francois Denoux	The father
Mme. Andre Wick	The mother
Youl Bryner	Jacques Hury
Pierre Claudel	The mayor
Georges Pitoeff, Jr.	Apprentice

Staging by Ludmilla Pitoeff; scenery by Simon Lissim; costumes by Mme. Pierre Claudel. (Given in French—the English version *The Tidings Brought to Mary* had formerly been presented by the Theater Guild.)

THE MOON VINE by Patricia Coleman

Opened February 11, 1943, at the Morosco Theater
Cast:

Vera Allen .... Mrs. Meade
Grace Coppin .... Strother Meade
Kate McComb......................... Miss Lucy Telfar
Agnes Scott Yost .... Mrs. Sylvaine
Robert Albury .... Larkin
Drop Dead .... Drop Dead
Phyllis Tyler..................... Miss Francie Taylor
Will Geer..................... Uncle Yancey Sylvaine
Richard Tyler............................. Zack Meade
Ruth Anderson .... Mattie
Phillip Bourneuf........................... Ovid Carter
Haila Stoddard .... Mariah Meade
Mary Lou Taylor...................... Ellen Hatfield
Arthur Franz .... Danny Hatfield
Donald Murphy .... Porter
Michael Road .... Fane
Youl Bryner.. André
A. Winfield Hoeny........... Brother Walt Littlejohn
John McKee .... The Rev. Dr. Randolph Hatfield
Biddy Fleet... Nic
Elmer Snowden...................................... Pic

Produced and directed by Jack Kirkland; staged by John
Cromwell; settings and costumes by Lucinda Ballard.

LUTE SONG (Based on classic Chinese drama *Pi-Pi-Ki*)

Opened February 6, 1946, at the Plymouth Theater
Cast:

Clarence Derwent ..... The manager/The Honorable
Tchang
Yul Brynner .... Tsai-Yong
Augustin Duncan .... Tsai, the father
Mildred Dunnock .... Madame Tsai, the mother
Mary Martin .... Tchao-ou-Niang
McKay Norris .... Prince Nieou, the Imperial
Preceptor
Helen Craig .... Princess Nieou-Chi
Nancy Davis .... Si-Tchun
Ralph Clanton .... The Genie
Other principals: Pamela Wilde, Sydelle Sylovna,
Blanche Zohar, Mary Ann Reeve, Diane de Brett,
Jack Amoroso, Gene Galvin, Max Leavitt, Bob
Turner, Tom Emlyn Williams, John Robert Lord,
John High, Gordon Showalter, Ronald Fletcher,
Lisa Maslova, Lisan Kay, Joseph Camiolo, Leslie
Rheinfeld

Directed by John Houseman; music by Sidney Howard and
Will Irwin; scenery and costumes by Robert Edmond Jones;
presented by Michael Myerberg.

DARK EYES by Elena Miramova in collaboration with Eugenie Leontovich

Opened March 24, 1984, at the Strand Theatre (London) Cast:

Bill Staughton .... Larry Field
Norris Smith .... Willoughby
May Carey .... Grandmother Field
Gladys Taylor .... Pearl
Genine Graham .... Helen Field
Yul Brynner .... Prince Nikolai Toradje
Dolly Rowles .... Natasha Rapakovich
Irina Baronova .... Tonia Karpova
Eugenia Delarova .... Olga Shimilevskya
Edwin Styles .... John Field

Directed by Charles Goldner; presented by Linnit and Dunfee Ltd. in association with Davis and Severn.

THE KING AND I (Based on the novel *Anna and the King of Siam* by Margaret Landon)

Opened March 29, 1951, at the St. James Theater
Cast:

Charles Francis	Captain Orton
Sandy Kennedy	Louis Leonowens
Gertrude Lawrence	Anna Leonowens
Leonard Graves	The Interpreter
John Juliana	The Kralahome
Yul Brynner	The King
Len Mence	Phra Alack
Doretta Morrow	Tuptim
Dorothy Sarnoff	Lady Thiang
Johnny Stewart	Prince Chulalongkorn
Baayork Lee	Princess Ying Yaowalak
Larry Douglas	Lun Tha
Robin Craven	Sir Edward Ramsay

Music by Richard Rodgers; book and lyrics by Oscar Hammerstein 2nd; staged by John van Druten; settings by Jo Mielziner; costumes by Irene Sharaff; choreography by Jerome Robbins; presented by Rogers and Hammerstein.

HOME SWEET HOMER (*Odysseus*) (Based on Homer's *Odyssey*)

Opened January 4, 1976, at the Palace Theater
Cast:

Yul Brynner	Odysseus
Joan Diener	Penelope
Russ Thatcher	Telamachus
Martin Vidnovic	Antinous
Ian Sullivan	Polyphemus
Bill Mackay	Ktesippos
Daniel Brown	Eurymachus
Brian Destazio	Leokritos
John Aristides	Pimteus
Bill Nabel	Mulios
Diana Davila	Nausikkaa

Music by Mitch Lee; book by Roland Kibbee and Albert Marre; lyrics by Charles Rurr and Forman Brown; presented by the John F. Kennedy Center for the Performing Arts.

THE KING AND I (Revival)

Opened May 2, 1977, at the Uris Theater
Cast:

Larry Swansen	Captain Orton
Alan Amick	Louis Leonowens
Constance Towers	Anna Leonowens
Jae Woo Lee	The Interpreter
Michael Kermoyan	The Kralahome
Yul Brynner	The King
June Angela	Tuptim
Hve-Young-Choi	Lady Thiang
Gene Profanato	Prince Chulalongkorn
Julie Woo	Princess Ying Yaowalak
Martin Vidnovic	Lun Tha
John Michael King	Sir Edward Ramsay

Music by Richard Rodgers; book and lyrics by Oscar Hammerstein 2nd; settings by Peter Wolf; costumes by Stanley Simmons; choreography by Jerome Robbins; directed by Yuriko; presented by Lee Gruber and Shelly Gross.

THE KING AND I (Revival)

Opened January 7, 1985, at the Broadway Theater
Cast:

Jeffrey Bryan Davis .... Louis Leonowens
Burt Edwards........................... Captain Orton
Mary Beth Piel .... Anna Leonowens
Jae Woo Lee........................... The Interpreter
Jonathan Farwell .... The Kralahome
Yul Brynner .... The King
Kathy Lee Brynner .... Lead royal dancer and Eliza
Sal Provenza................................. Lun Tha
Patricia Welch .... Tuptim
Irma-Estel LaGuerre .... Lady Thiang
Araby Abava.................. Prince Chulalongkorn
Yvette Laura Martin........ Princess Ying Yaowalak
Patricia Weber.............................. Fan dancer
Edward Crotty.................... Sir Edward Ramsay
Hope Sogawa .... Uncle Thomas
Evelina Deocares .... Little Eva
Deborah Harada .... Topsy
Rebecca West .... Simon
Patricia Weber..................................... Angel

Music by Richard Rodgers; book and lyrics by Oscar Hammerstein 2nd; produced and directed by Mitch Lee; choreography by Rebecca West; settings by Peter Wolf; costumes
by Stanley Simmons; presented by Mitch Lee.

Film Chronology

PORT OF NEW YORK (1949) Based on story by Arthur Ross and Bert Murray

Studio: Eagle-Lion
Cast:

Scott Brady	Mickey Walters
Richard Rober	Jim Flannery
K.T. Stevens	Toni Camden
Yul Brynner	Paul Vicola
Arthur Blake	Dolly Carney
Lynne Carter	Lili Long
John Kellog	Lenny
William Challee	Leo Stasser

Producer: Aubrey Schenck; associate producer: James Vaughn; director: Laslo Benedek; screenplay: Eugene Ling; additional dialogue: Leo Townsend; art direction: Edward Ilou; photography: George Diskant; music: Sol Kaplan; musical direction: Irving Friedman; editor: Norman Colbert; running time: 87 minutes.

THE TEN COMMANDMENTS (1956)*

Studio: Paramount
Cast:

Charlton Heston .... Moses
Yul Brynner .... Rameses
Anne Baxter .... Nefertiri
Yvonne De Carlo .... Sephora
Edward G. Robinson .... Dathan
Sir Cedric Hardwicke .... Sethi
Debra Paget .... Lilia
John Derek .... Joshua
Nina Foch .... Bithia
Judith Anderson .... Memnet
John Carradine .... Aaron
Vincent Price .... Baka
Martha Scott .... Yochabel
Olive Deering .... Miriam
Douglas Dumbrille .... Jannes
Henry Wilcoxon .... Pentaur
H.B. Warner .... Amminadab
Francis McDonald .... Simon
Tommy Doran .... Gershom
Ian Keith .... Rameses I

Producer: Cecil B. DeMille; associate producer: Henry Wilcoxon; director: Cecil B. DeMille; screenplay: Aeneas MacKenzie, Jesse L. Lasky, Jr., Jack Gariss, Frederic M. Frank; photography: Loval Griggs, John Warren, Wallace Kelley, J. Peverell Marley; editor: Anne Bauchens; art direction: Hall Pereira, Walter Tyler, Albert Nozaki; set direction: Sam Comer, Ray Mover; music: Elmer Bernstein; special effects: John Fulton; sound: Loren Ryder, Louis Mesenkop, Harry Lindgren, Gene Garvin; choreography: Leroy Prinz, Ruth Godfrey; cos-

---

*Although filmed before *The King and I*, was released later.

tumes: Edith Head, Ralph Jester, John Jenson, Dorothy Jenkins, Arnold Friberg; makeup: Wally Westmore, Frank Westmore, Frank McCoy; hairstyles: Nellie Manley; unit director: Arthur Rosson; running time: 219 minutes.

THE KING AND I (1956) Based on book *Anna and the King of Siam* by Margaret Landon. Also the play *The King and I* by Rodgers and Hammerstein

Studio: 20th Century-Fox
Cast:

Deborah Kerr	Anna Leonowens
Yul Brynner	The King
Rita Moreno	Tuptim
Terry Saunders	Lady Thiang
Rex Thompson	Louis Leonowens
Martin Benson	The Kralahome
Leonard Strong	The Interpreter
Carlos Rivas	Lun Tha
Patrick Adiarte	Prince Chulalongkorn
Alan Mowbray	British Ambassador
Geoffrey Toone	Ramsay

Producer: Charles Brackett; director: Walter Lang; music: Richard Rodgers; lyrics and book: Oscar Hammerstein 2nd; screenplay: Ernest Lehman; choreography: Jerome Robbins; photography: Leon Shamroy; editor: Robert Simpson; art direction: John DeCuir, Lyle Wheeler; set direction: Walter Scott, Paul Fox; costumes: Irene Sharaff; music director: Alfred Newman, Ken Darby; running time: 133 minutes.

ANASTASIA (1956) Based on Guy Botan's adaptation of a play by Marcelle Maurette

Studio: 20th Century-Fox
Cast:

> *Ingrid Bergman* .... Anastasia/Anna Anderson
> *Yul Brynner* .... Bounine
> *Helen Hayes* .... The Dowager Empress
> *Akim Tamiroff* .... Chernov
> *Maritita Hunt* .... Baroness von Livenbaum
> *Gregoire Gromoff* .... Stepan
> *Sacha Piteoff* .... Petrovin
> *Ivan Desny* .... Prince Paul
> *Felix Aylmer* .... Russian Chamberlain
> *Natalie Schafer* .... Lissenskaia
> *Katel Stepanek* .... Vlados
> *Ina de la Haye* .... Marusla

Producer: Buddy Adler; director: Anatole Litvak; screenplay: Arthur Laurents; photography: Jack Hilyard; music: Alfred Newman; art direction: Andrei Andrew, Bill Andrews; sound: Carl Faulkner; editor: Bert Bates; costumes: Rene Hubert; running time: 105 minutes.

THE BROTHERS KARAMAZOV (1958) Based on the novel by Fyodor Dostoyevsky

Studio: Metro-Goldwyn-Mayer
Cast:

Yul Brynner	Dmitri Karamazov
Maria Schell	Grushenka
Claire Bloom	Katya
Lee J. Cobb	Fyodor Karamazov
Richard Basehart	Ivan Karamazov
Albert Salmi	Smerdyakov
Judith Evelyn	Mme. Anna Hohlakov
Harry Townes	Ippolit Kirillov
Edgar Stehli	Gregory
Miko Oscard	Illusha Snegiryov
David Opatoshu	Captain Snegiryov
William Shatner	Alexey Karamazov
Mel Welles	Trifon Borissovitch
Simon Oakland	Mavrayek
Frank de Kova	Captain Vrublevski
Jay Adler	Pawnbroker
Ann Morrison	Marya
Gage Clarke	Defense counsel

Producer: Pandro Berman; associate producer: Kathryn Hereford; director: Richard Brooks; screenplay: Richard Brooks; photography: John Alton; editor: John Dunning; art direction: William Horning, Paul Grosse; set direction: Henry Grace, Robert Priestley; music: Bronislau Kaper; costumes: Walter Plunkett; hair styles: Sydney Guilaroff; makeup: William Tuttle; special effects: Lee LeBlanc; color consultant: Charles Hagedon; assistant director: William Shanks; recording supervisor: Wesley Miller; technical adviser: Andrey Tolstoy; running time: 146 minutes.

THE BUCCANEER (1958) Based on Jeannie Macpherson's adaptation of the book *Lafitte the Pirate* by Lyle Saxon

Studio: Paramount
Cast:

Yul Brynner	Jean Lafitte
Charlton Heston	General Andrew Jackson
Claire Bloom	Bonnie Brown
Charles Boyer	Dominique You
Henry Hull	Ezra Peavey
Inger Stevens	Annette Clairborne
E.G. Marshall	Governor Clairborne
Lorne Greene	Mercier
Jerry Hartleben	Miggs
Ted DeCorsia	Captain Rumbo
Woodrow Strode	Toro

Introduction and prologue by Cecil B. DeMille
Supervisor: Cecil B. DeMille; producer: Henry Wilcoxon; director: Anthony Quinn; screenplay: Jesse L. Lasky, Jr., Bernice Mosk, Harold Lamb, Edwin Justus Mayer, J. Gardner Sullivan; photography: Loyal Griggs, John Fulton, Paul Lerpae, Farciot Edouart, Wallace Kelley; editor: Archie Marshek; color consultant: Richard Mueller; art direction: Hall Pereira, Walter Tyler, Albert Nozaki; set direction: Sam Comer, Ray Moyer; music: Elmer Bernstein; choreography: Josephene Earle; costumes: Edith Head, Ralph Jester, John Jensen, Rebecca Morelli; makeup: Wally Westmore; hairstyles: Nellie Manley; sound: Harry Lindgren, Winston Leverett; technical adviser: Captain A.T. Ostrander; unit director: Arthur Rosson; running time: 120 minutes.

THE JOURNEY (1959)

Studio: Metro-Goldwyn-Mayer
Cast:

Deborah Kerr	Lady Diana Ashmore
Yul Brynner	Major Surov
Jason Robards, Jr.	Paul Kedes
Robert Morley	Hugh Deverill
E.G. Marshall	Harold Rhinelander
Anne Jackson	Margie Rhinelander
Kurt Kasznar	Csepege
David Kossoff	Simon Avron
Gerard Oury	Teklel Hafouli
Marie Daems	Francoise Hafouli
Anouk Aimee	Eva
Ronny Howard	Billy Rhinelander

Producer: Anatole Litvak; director: Anatole Litvak; screenplay: George Tabori; photography: Jack Hildyard, John Kotze; editor: Dorothy Spencer; art direction: Werner Schlichting, Isabella Schlichting; music: Georges Auric, Michael Michelet; sound: Kurt Schwarz, John Cox; costumes: Rene Hubert; makeup: David Aylott, Eric Allwright; hairstyles: Gordon Bond; technical advisers: Moura Budgberg, Tibor Simanyi, Georg Daniloff; union director: Noel Howard; assistant producer: Carl Czokoll; assistant director: Gerold O'Hara; running time: 123 minutes.

THE SOUND AND THE FURY (1959) Based on the novel by William Faulkner

Studio: 20th Century-Fox
Cast:

Yul Brynner	Jason
Joanne Woodward	Quentin
Margaret Leighton	Caddy
Stuart Whitman	Charles Busch
Ethel Waters	Dilsey
Jack Warden	Ben
John Beal	Howard
Albert Dekker	Earl Snopes
Francoise Rosay	Mrs. Compson
Stephen Perry	Luster
Esther Dale	Mrs. Mansfield
Adrian Martin	Effie Mansfield
Roy Glenn	Job
William Gunn	T.P.

Producer: Jerry Wald; director: Martin Ritt; screenplay: Irving Ravetch, Harriet Frank, Jr.; music: Alex North, Edward Powell; editor: Stuart Gilmore; photography: Charles Clarke; art direction: Lyle Wheeler, Maurice Ransford; set direction: Walter Scott, Paul Fox; sound: Charles Peck, Harry Leonard; wardrobe designer: Charles LeMaire; costumes: Adele Palmer; makeup: Ben Nye; hairstyles: Helen Turpin; color consultant: Leonard Doss; assistant director: Eli Dunn; running time: 115 minutes.

LE TESTAMENT D'ORPHÉE Filmed in France

E.C. Production released by Films Around the World
Cast:

Jean Cocteau .... Jean Cocteau
Jean Marais .... Oedipus
Edouard Dermit .... Cegeste
Marie Casares .... The Princess
Claudine Oger .... Pallas Athens
Supporting players: Pablo Picasso, Yul Brynner,
Luis Dominguin, Serge Lifar, Hans Warner,
Mme. Picasso, Lucia Bose, Michele Lemoine,
Françoise Sagan.

Producer: Jean Thulliter; director: Jean Cocteau; screenplay:
Jean Cocteau; photography: R. Pontoiseau; assistant director:
Pierre Resnick; running time: 79 minutes.

SOLOMON AND SHEBA (1959) Based on a story by Crane Wilbur

Studio: United Artists
Cast:

Yul Brynner	Solomon
Gina Lollobrigida	Sheba
George Sanders	Adonijah
Marisa Pavan	Abishag
John Crawford	Joab
Finlay Currie	King David
Lawrence Naismith	Hezrai
Jose Nieto	Ahab
David Farrar	Pharoah
Alejandro Rey	Sittar
Harry Andrews	Baltor
Jack Gwillim	Josiah
Julio Pena	Zadok
Maruchi Fresno	Bathsheba
William Devlin	Nathan
Jean Anderson	Takyan

Producer: Ted Richmond; director: King Vidor; screenplay: Anthony Veiller, Paul Dudley, George Bruce; photography: Freddie Young, John Von Kotze; editor: John Ludwig; music: Mario Nascimbene; art direction: Richard Day, Alfred Sweeney; sound: F.C. Hughesdon, Aubrey Lewis, David Hildyard; choreography: Jaroslav Berger; special effects: Alex Weldon; costumes: Emilo Schuberth, Eric Seelig, Pearl Miller; makeup: John O'Gorman, Tom Lee, Tom Tuttle; technical advisers: Augustin Medina, Kenny Lee; unit director: Noël Coward; assistant directors: Piero Mussetta, Pepe Lopez; running time: 139 minutes.

ONCE MORE WITH FEELING (1960) Based on play by Harry Kurnitz

Studio: Columbia Pictures
Cast:

Yul Brynner	Victor Fabian
Kay Kendall	Dolly Fabian
Gregory Ratoff	Maxwell Archer
Geoffrey Toone	Dr. Hilliard
Maxwell Shaw	Gendel
Mervyn Johns	Mr. Wilbur, Jr.
Martin Benson	Bardini
Harry Lockhart	Chester
C.E. Joy	Sir Austin Flapp
Shirley Ann Field	Angela Hopper
Grace Newcombe	Mrs. Wilbur
C.S. Stuart	Manning

Producer: Stanley Donen; associate producer: Paul Radin; director: Stanley Donen; screenplay: Harry Kurnitz; music: Chopin, Beethoven, Liszt, Rimsky-Korsakoff, Strauss, Tchaikovsky, Wagner, Sousa; conductor: Muir Mathieson; photography: Georges Perinal; editor: Jack Harris; sound: Joseph DeBretagne; wardrobe: Givenchy; makeup: Eric Allwright, Jean Paul Ulysee; assistant director: Paul Feyder; running time: 92 minutes.

SURPRISE PACKAGE (1960) Based on the novel *A Gift from the Boys* by Art Buchwald

Studio: Columbia Pictures
Cast:

Yul Brynner	Nico March
Mitzi Gaynor	Gabby Rogers
Noël Coward	King Pavell II
Man Mountain Dean	Igor Trofim
Guy Deghy	Tibor Smolny
Lyndon Brook	Stavrin
Eric Pohlman	Stefan Miralis
George Coulouris	Dr. Hugo Palmer
Lionel Murton	1st US Marshall
Barry Foster	2nd US Marshall
Warren Mitchell	Klimatis
Bill Nagy	Johnny Stettina

Producer: Stanley Donen; director: Stanley Donen; photography: Christopher Challis; editor: James Clarke; music: Benjamin Frankel; sound: John Cox, George Stephenson, Bob Jones; wardrobe: Mattli; makeup: John O'Gorman, Eric Allwright.

THE MAGNIFICENT SEVEN (1960) Based on Akira Kurosawa's film *Seven Samurai*

Studio: Mirisch-Alpha
Cast:

Yul Brynner	Chris
Eli Wallach	Calvera
Steve McQueen	Vin
Charles Bronson	O'Reilly
Robert Vaughn	Lee
James Coburn	Britt
Horst Bucholz	Chico
Brad Dexter	Harry Luck
Vladimir Sokoloff	Old man

Producer: John Sturges; director: John Sturges; screenplay: William Roberts; editor: Ferris Webster; music: Elmer Bernstein; art direction: Edward Fitzgerald; set direction: Rafael Suarez; sound: Jack Solomon, Rafael Esparza; makeup: Emile LaVigne, Daniel Strispeke; special effects: Milt Rice; production manager: Chico Day; assistant directors: Robert Relyea, Jaime Contreras; running time: 128 minutes.

ESCAPE FROM ZAHRAIN (1962) Based on the novel *Appointment in Zahrain* by Michael Barrett

Studio: Paramount
Cast:

Yul Brynner	Sharif
Sal Mineo	Ahmed
Jack Warden	Huston
Madlyn Rhue	Laila
Tony Caruso	Tahar
Jay Novello	Hassan
Leonard Strong	Ambulance driver
James Mason	Johnson

Producer: Ronald Neame; associate producer: Chico Day; director: Ronald Neame; screenplay: Robins Estridge; photography: Ellsworth Fredricks, Irwin Roberts, John Fulton; editor: Eda Warren; music: Lyn Murray; art direction: Eddie Imazu; sound: Gene Merritt, Charles Grenzbach; assistant director: Tom Connors, Jr.; running time: 93 minutes.

TARAS BULBA (1962) Based on novel by Nikolai Gogol

Studio: United Artists
Cast:

Tony Curtis	Andrei Bulba
Yul Brynner	Taras Bulba
Christine Kaufman	Natalia Dubrov
Sam Wanamaker	Filipenko
Brad Dexter	Shilo
Guy Rolfe	Prince Grigory
Vladimir Sokoloff	Old Stephan
Ilka Windish	Sophia Bulba
Perry Lopez	Ostap Bulba
George Macready	Governor

Producer: Harold Hecht; director: J. Lee Thompson; screenplay: Waldo Salt, Karl Tunberg; photography: Joseph MacDonald, Howard Anderson, Russ Lawson; editors: William Reynolds, Gene Milford, Eda Warren; music: Franz Waxman; art direction: Edward Carrere; set direction: William Calvert; sound: Stan Cooley, Bert Mallberg; special effects: Fred Wolff, Barney Wolf; costumes: Norma Koch; makeup: Frank McCoy, Emile Lavigne, Daniel Strispeke; hairstyles: Joan St. Oegger; assistant director: Tom Shaw; running time: 122 minutes.

KINGS OF THE SUN (1963) Based on a story by Elliott Arnold

Studio: Mirsch Productions
Cast:

Yul Brynner	Black Eagle
George Chakiris..................................	Balam
Shirley Anne Field	Ixchel
Richard Basehart	Ah Min
Brad Dexter...................................	Ah Haleb
Barry Morse	Ah Zok
Leo Gordon	Humac Ceel
Armando Silverstre	Isatai
Rudy Solar..	Pitz
Victoria Vettri..................................	Ixzubin

Producer: Lewis Rachmil; director: J. Lee Thompson; screenplay: Elliott Arnold, James Webb; photography: Joseph MacDonald; music: Elmer Bernstein; editor: William Reynold; art director: Alfred Ybarra; sound: Bert Hallberg; special effects: Roscoe Cline; costumes: Norma Koch; makeup: Emile LaVigne; hairstyles: Mary Babcock; unit manager: Robert Relyea; assistant producer: Allen Wood; assistant director: Tom Shaw; running time: 108 minutes.

FLIGHT FROM ASHIYA (1964) Based on the novel by Elliott Arnold

Studio: Daiei Motion Picture Company and Harold Hecht Films
Cast:

Yul Brynner	Sgt. Mike Takashima
Richard Widmark	Col. Glenn Stevenson
George Chakiris	Lt. John Gregg
Suzy Parker	Lucille Carroll
Shirley Knight	Caroline Gordon
Eiko Taki	Tomiko
Daniele Gaubert	Leila
Joe De Reda	Sgt. Randy Smith
Mitsuhiro Sugiyama	Charlie

Producer: Harold Hecht; director: Michael Anderson; screenplay: Elliott Arnold, Waldo Salt; photography: Joseph MacDonald, Burnett Guffey; editor: Gordon Pilkington; art direction: Tom Shimogawara; music: Frank Cordell; sound: Masao Osumi; assistant director: Milton Feldman; running time: 100 minutes.

INVITATION TO A GUNFIGHTER (1964) Based on a story by Hal Goodman and Larry Klein

Studio: A Stanley Kramer Production released by United Artists
Cast:

Yul Brynner	Jules Gaspart D'Estaing
Janice Rule	Ruth Adams
George Segal	Matt Weaver
Pat Hingle	Sam Brewster
Brad Dexter	Kenarsie
Alfred Ryder	Doc Barker
Mike Kellin	Tom
Clifford Davis	Crane Adams
Curt Conway	McKeever
Clifton James	Tuttle
Bert Freed	Sheriff
Clarke Gordon	Hickman

Producer: Richard Wilson; director: Richard Wilson; screenplay: Richard and Elizabeth Wilson; photography: Joe McDonald; editor: Bob Jones; art direction: Robert Clatworthy; music: David Raskin; sound: William Russell; technical adviser: Rodd Redwing; production manager: Ivan Volkman; assistant director: Austin Jewell; running time: 91 minutes.

THE SABOTEUR: CODE NAME—MORITURI (1965) Based
on the novel by Werner Joerg Luedecke

Studio: 20th Century-Fox
Cast:

Marlon Brando .... Robert Crain
Yul Brynner .... Captain Mueller
Janet Margolin .... Esther
Trevor Howard .... Colonel Statter
Wally Cox................................. Dr. Ambach
Martin Benrath.................................... Kruse
Max Haufier .... Branner
Rainer Penkert................................ Milkereit
William Redfield............................... Baldwin
Hans Christian Blech .... Donkeyman

Producer: Aaron Rosenberg; director: Bernhard Wicki;
screenplay: Daniel Taradash; photography: Joseph Silver; editor: Joseph Silver; sound: Garry Harris; music: Jerry Gold-
smith; art direction: Jack Smith, Herman Blumenthal; assistant
director: David Silver; running time: 120 minutes.

THE POPPY IS ALSO A FLOWER (1966) Based on a story idea by Ian Flemming

Studio: A Telson UN Production (alphabetical listing)
Cast:

Santa Berger	Nightclub entertainer
Stephen Boyd	Benson
Yul Brynner	Colonel Salem
Angie Dickinson	Linda
Georges Geret	Superintendent Roche
Hugh Griffith	Tribal Chief
Jack Hawkins	General Bahar
Rita Hayworth	Monique
Trevor Howard	Lincoln
Jocelyn Lane	Photographer
Trini Lopez	Trini Lopez
E.G. Marshall	Jones
Marcello Mastroianni	Inspector Mosca
Amedeoi Nazzari	Captain Dinonno
Jean-Claude Pascal	Tribesman Leader
Anthony Quale	Captain Moore
Gilbert Roland	Marco
Harold Sakata	Martin
Omar Sharif	Dr. Rad
Barry Sullivan	Chasen
Nedja Tiller	Dr. Bronovska
Eli Wallach	Locamo
Howard Veron	Police analyst

Producer: Euan Lloyd; director: Terence Young; screenplay: Jo Eisinger; photography: Henri Alekan, Tony Brown; editors: Monique Bonnot, Peter Thornton, Henry Richardson; music: Georges Auric; art direction: Maurice Colasson, Tony Roman; set direction: Freda Pearson; special effects: Paul Pollard; sound: Jean Monchablan; running time: 100 minutes.

CAST A GIANT SHADOW (1966) Based on book by Ted Berkman

Studio: Mirisch-Lienroc-Batiac Productions
Cast:

Kirk Douglas	Col. David (Mickey) Marcus
Senta Berger	Magda Simon
Angie Dickinson	Emma Marcus
Haym Topal	Abou Ibn Kader
Luther Adler	Jacob Zion
Stathis Giallelis	Ram Oren
James Donald	Safir
Yul Brynner	Asher Goren
John Wayne	General Mike Randolph
Frank Sinatra	Vince
Gary Merrill	Pentagon Chief of Staff

Producer: Melville Shavelson; coproducer: Michael Wayne; director: Melville Shavelson; screenplay: Melville Shavelson; photography: Aldo Tonti; editors: Bert Bates, Gene Ruggiero; music: Elmer Bernstein; technical adviser: Nathan Yadan; assistant directors: Jack Reddish, Charles Scrott, Jr., Tim Zimmerman; running time: 141 minutes.

RETURN OF THE SEVEN (1966) Filmed in Spain

Studio: Co-Production—Mirisch and C.B. Films
Cast:

Yul Brynner	Chris
Robert Fuller	Vin
Julian Mateos	Chico
Jordan Christopher	Manuel
Claude Akins	Frank
Warren Oates	Colbee
Elisa Montes	Petra
Fernando Rey	Priest
Emilio Fernandez	Lorea
Rudy Acosta	Lopez
Virgilio Texera	Luis

Producer: Ted Richmond; associate producer: Robert Goodstein; director: Burt Kennedy; screenplay: Larry Cohen; photography: Paul Vogel; music: Elmer Bernstein; editor: Bert Bates; art direction: Jose Alguero; set direction: Antonio Mateos; sound: Jonathan Bates, J.B. Smith; special effects: Dick Parker; wardrobe: Eric Seelig; makeup: Jose Maria Sanchez; production supervisor: Allen Wood; assistant director: Jose Lopez Radero; running time: 95 minutes.

TRIPLE CROSS (1967) Based on book *The Eddie Chapman Story* by Frank Owen

Studio: Cineurop, released by Warner Brothers
Cast:

Christopher Plummer .... Eddie Chapman
Yul Brynner .... Baron von Grunen
Romy Schneider .... The Countess
Trevor Howard .... The distinguished civilian
Claudine Auger................................. Paulette
Gert Frobe.......................... Colonel Steinhager
Harry Meyen .... Lt. Keller
Jean-Claude Barco..................... Major von Leeb
Robert Favart .... General Dalrymple
Hans.................................. Frank Letterman

Producer: Jacques-Paul Bertrand; director: Terence Young; screenplay: Rene Hardy, William Marchant; photography: Henri Alekan; editor: Roger Dwyre; music: Georges Garvarentz; art direction: Tony Roman; sound: Jacques Lebreton, Johnny Dwyre; production managers: Jean Vetter, Pierre Laurent, Dennis Hall; assistant directors: Christian Raoux, Bernard Quatrehomme; running time: 126 minutes.

THE LONG DUEL (1967) Based on a book by Ranveer Singh

Studio: A Rank Production
Cast:

Yul Brynner	Sultan
Trevor Howard	Freddy Young
Harry Andrews	Superintendent Stafford
Charlotte Rampling	Jane Stafford
Andrew Keir	Gungarem
Virginia North	Champa
Paul Hardwick	Jamadar
Laurence Naismith	McDougal
Imogen Hassall	Tara
Maurice Denham	Governor
Antonio Ruiz	Munnu

Producer: Ken Annakin; associate producers: Frank Sherwin Green, Aida Young; director: Ken Annakin; screenplay: Peter Yeldham; photography: Jack Hildyard; editor: Bert Bates; music: Patrick John Scott; art direction: Alex Vetchinsky; set direction: Arthur Taksen; special effects: Dick Parker; sound: Dudley Messenger, Ken Barker; costumes: John Furniss; assistant director: Clive Reed; production managers: Gregorio Sacristan, Bernard Hanson; running time: 115 minutes.

THE BATTLE ON THE RIVER NERETVA (1968) Filmed in Yugoslavia

Studio: Released by American International Films
Cast:

Yul Brynner	Partisan Vlado
Sergei Bondarchuk	Martin
Curt Jurgens	General Lohring
Silva Koscina	Danica
Orson Welles	Senator
Hardy Kruger	Colonel Kranzer
Milena Dravic	Nada
Lojze Roman	Commander Ivan
Franco Nero	Captain Riva
Ljubisa Samardjic	Novak

Producer: Veljko Bulajic (U.S. version—Steve Previn); director: Veljko Bulajic; screenplay: Ratko Djurovic, Stevo Bulajic, Veljko Bulajic, Ugo Pirro, Alfred Weidenmann; English adaptation: Alfred Hayes; photography: Tomislav Pinter; editors: Roger Dwyer, Vanja Benjas; music: Vladimir Kraus-Rajteric, Bernard Harrman; art direction: Dusko Jericevic, Vladimir Tadej; special effects: Zfravko Smojver, Zoran Dordenc; sound: Jean Neny, Alex Pront; production manager: Zfravko Mihalic; running time: 175 minutes.

THE DOUBLE MAN (1968) Based on novel *Legacy of a Spy* by Henry Maxfield

Studio: An Albion Production
Cast:

Yul Brynner	Dan Slater/Kalmar
Britt Ekland	Gina Ericson
Clive Revill	Frank Wheatly
Moira Lister	Mrs. Carrington
Lloyd Nolan	Bill Edwards
Anton Diffring	Colonel Berthold
George Mikell	Max Gruner
Brandon Brady	Gregori
David Healy	Halstead

Producer: Hal Chester; director: Franklin Schaffner; screenplay: Frank Tarloff, Alfred Haynes; photography: Denys Coop; editor: Richard Best; music: Ernie Freeman, Stanley Black; art direction: Arthur Lawson; set direction: David Bill; sound: A.W. Lumkin, Tony Wolf, Len Shilton; wardrobe for Moira Lister: Christian Dior; costumes: Cortney Elliott; production manager: L.C. Rudkin; assistant directors: Ron Jackson, William Cartlidge; running time: 105 minutes.

VILLA RIDES (1968) Based on the book *Pancho Villa* by William Douglas Lansford

Studio: Paramount
Cast:

Yul Brynner	Villa
Robert Mitchum	Lee Arnold
Grazia Buccella	Fina
Charles Bronson	Fierro
Herbert Lom	Huerta
Alexander Knox	President Madero
Robert Viharo	Urbina
Frank Wolff	Ramirez
Fernando Rey	Fuentes
Antonio Ruiz	Juan
Diana Lorys	Emilita
Andres Monreal	Herrera
Regina de Julian	Lupita

Producer: Ted Richmond; director: Buzz Kulik; screenplay: Robert Towne, Sam Peckinpah; photography: Jack Hildyard; editor: David Bretherton; music: Maurice Jarre; sound: Roy Charman; assistant director: Tony Fuentes; running time: 125 minutes.

THE FILE OF THE GOLDEN GOOSE (1969) Based on a story by John Higgins

Studio: Carolan-Dador Production released by United Artists
Cast:

Yul Brynner	Novak
Charles Gray	Owl
Edward Woodward	Thompson
Bernard Archerd	Collins
John Barrie	Sloane
Ivor Doan	Reynolds
Anthony Jacobs	Firenos
Adrienne Corri	Tina
Karel Stepanek	Mueller
Walter Gotell	Leeds
Hilary Dwyer	Anne

Producer: David Rose; director: Sam Wanamaker; screenplay: John Higgins, James Gordon; photography: Ken Hodges; editor: Oswald Hafenrichter; art direction: George Provis; sound: Ken Ritchie; production manager: Pat Green; assistant director: Ray Fritt; running time: 105 minutes.

THE MADWOMAN OF CHAILLOT (1969) Based on play by
Jean Giraudoux, adapted by Maurice Volency

Studio: Warner Brothers-Seven Arts
Cast:

Katharine Hepburn	Countess Aurelia
Charles Boyer	The Broker
Claude Dauphin	Dr. Jadin
Edith Evans	Josephine
John Gavin	The Reverend
Yul Brynner	The Chairman
Paul Henreid	The General
Oscar Homolka	The Commissar
Margaret Leighton	Constance
Giulietta Masina	Gabrielle
Richard Chamberlain	Roderick
Nanette Newman	Irma
Donald Pleasence	The Prospector
Danny Kaye	The Ragpicker
Gordon Heath	The Folksinger
Gerald Sim	Julius
Fernand Gravey	Police sergeant

Producer: Ely Landau; director: Bryan Forbes; screenplay:
Edward Archalt; photography: Claude Renoir, Burnett Guffey; editor: Roger Dwyre; music: Michael Lewis; art direction:
Georges Petitot; sound: Janet Davidson; running time: 140
minutes.

THE MAGIC CHRISTIAN* (1970) Based on a novel by
Terry Southern

Studio: Commonwealth United Production
Cast:

> Peter Sellers, Ringo Starr, Wilfrid Hyde White,
> Richard Attenborough, Laurence Harvey, Chris-
> topher Lee, Spike Milligan, Roman Polanski, Ra-
> quel Welch, Isobel Jeans, Victor Madden, Peter
> Graves

Producer: Dennis O'Dell; director: Joseph McGrath; screenplay: Terry Southern, Joseph McGrath, Peter Sellers; photography: Geoffrey Unsworth; editor: Kevin Connor; art
direction: George Djurkovic; costumes: Vangie Harrison;
choreography: Lionel Blair; sound: Brian Holland; special effects: Wally Veevers; assistant director: Roger Simons; running time: 92 minutes.

---

*Brynner disguised as cabaret songstress was not listed in the screen
credits.

ROMANCE OF A HORSETHIEF (1971) Based on a story by Joseph Opatoshu

Studio: Allied Artists
Cast:

Yul Brynner	Captain Stoloff
Eli Wallach	Kifke
Jane Birkin	Naomi
Oliver Tobias	Zanvill
David Opatoshu	Shloime
Lainie Kazan	Estusha
Serge Gainsbourg	Sigmund
Henri Sera	Mendel
Linda Veras	Countess Grabowsky
Vladimir Bacic	Gruber
Blanko Plesa	Lt. Vishinsky
Alenka Rancic	Sura

Producer: Gene Gutowski; director: Abraham Polonsky; screenplay: David Opatoshu; editor: Kevin Connor; music: Mort Shumma; costumes: Ruth Myers; production manager: George Reuther; running time: 100 minutes.

THE LIGHT AT THE EDGE OF THE WORLD (1971) Based on the novel by Jules Verne

Studio: Bryna Productions (Hollywood), and Jet Films (Madrid) and Triumfilm (Vaduz)
Cast:

Kirk Douglas	Denton
Yul Brynner	Kongre
Samantha Eggar	Arabella
Jean-Claude Drouot	Virgilio
Fernando Rey	Captain Moriz
Renalto Salvatori	Montefiore
Massimo Ranieri	Felipe
Aldo Sambrell	Tarcante
Tito Garcia	Emilio

Producer: Kirk Douglas; director: Kevin Billington; screenplay: Tom Rowe, Rachel Billington; photography: Henri Decae, Cecilio Paniagua; editor: Bert Bates; art direction: Enrique Alarcon; sound: A.J. Willis, Wally Milner, Enrique Molinero; costumes: Deirdre Clancy, Manuel Mampaso; makeup: Jose Antonio Sanchez, Ramon De Diego; hairstyles: Josefa Rubio; production manager: Francisco Romero; assistant director: Julio Sempere; running time: 101 minutes.

ADIOS SABATA (1971) Filmed in Italy

Studio: Alberto Grimaldi Production—released by United Artists
Cast:

Yul Brynner	Sabata
Dean Reed	Ballantine
Pedro Sanchez	Escudo
Joseph Persaud	Gitana
Gerard Herter	Colonel Skimmel
Salvatore Borgese	September
Franco Fantasia	Ocano
Salvatore Billa	Manuel
Gianni Rizzo	Folgen

Producer: Alberto Grimaldi; associate producer: Roberto Cocco; director: Frank Kramer; screenplay: Renato Izzo, Gianfranco Parolini; photography: Sandro Mancori; music: Bruno Nicolai; assistant director: Inazio Dolce; running time: 106 minutes.

CATLOW (1971) Filmed in Spain—Based on novel by Louis L'Amour

Studio: Metro-Goldwyn-Mayer
Cast:

Yul Brynner .... Catlow
Richard Crenna .... Cowan
Leonard Nimoy .... Miller
Jo Ann Pflug .... Christina
Deliah Lavi .... Rosita
Jeff Corey .... Merridew
Julian Mateos .... Recalde
Michael Delano .... Rio
David Ladd .... Caxton
Bessie Love .... Mrs. Frost

Producer: Euan Lloyd; director: Sam Wanamaker; screenplay: J.J. Griffith, Scot Finch; photography: Ted Scaife; editors: John Glen, Alan Killick; music: Roy Budd; art direction: Herbert Smith; sound: Wally Milner; assistant director: Jose Maria Ochoa; running time: 103 minutes.

FUZZ (1972) Based on the novel by Evan Hunter (Ed McBain)

Studio: United Artists
Cast:

Burt Reynolds	Steve Carella
Raquel Welch	Eileen McHenry
Yul Brynner	The deaf man
Jack Weston	Meyer Meyer
Peter Bonerz	Buck
Cal Bellini	Ahmad
Don Gordon	Anthony La Bresca
Steve Ihnat	Andy Parker
James McEachin	Arthur Brown

Producer: Jack Farren; director: Richard Colla; screenplay: Evan Hunter; editor: Robert Kimble; music: Dave Grusin; art direction: Hilyard Brown; sound: Barry Thomas; costumes: Dorothy Jeakins; makeup: Tom Ellingswood, Ed Butterworth; hairstyles: Jan Brunson; running time: 93 minutes.

LE SERPENT (1973) Based on the novel by Pierre Nord—
Filmed in France and West Germany

Studio: Les Films La Boetie-Euro International Rialto
Cast:

Yul Brynner	Viassov
Henry Fonda	Davies
Dirk Bogarde	Boyle
Philippe Noiret	Berthon
Michael Bouquet	Tavel
Farley Granger	Expert
Virna Lisi	Annabel Lee
Martin Held	Lepka
Robert Alda	Questioner
Elga Anderson	Kate
Natalie Nerval	Tatiana
Guy Trejan	Daval

Producer: Henri Verneuil; director: Henri Verneuil; screenplay: Henri Verneuil, Gilles Perrauit; photography: Claude
Renoir; editor: Pierre Gillete; music: Ennio Morricone; art
direction: Jacques Sauinier; running time: 120 minutes.

WESTWORLD (1973)

Studio: Metro-Goldwyn-Mayer
Cast:

Yul Brynner	Gunslinger
Richard Benjamin	Peter Martin
James Brolin	John Blane
Alan Oppenheimer	Chief supervisor
Dick Van Patten	Banker
Norman Bartold	Medieval Knight
Michael Mikler	Black Knight
Majel Barrett	Miss Carrie
Victoria Shaw	Queen
Wade Crosby	Bartender
Linda Scott	Arlette
Chris Holter	Stewardess
Charles Seel	Bellman

Producer: Paul Lazarus III; associate producer: Michael Rachmil; director: Michael Crichton; screenplay: Michael Crichton; photography: Gene Polito; editor: David Bretherton; music: Fred Karlin; art direction: Herman Blumenthal; set direction: John Austin; sound: Richard Church, Henry Tetrick; assistant director: Claude Binyon, Jr.; running time: 90 minutes.

FUTUREWORLD (1975)

Studio: American International Pictures
Cast:

Peter Fonda	Chuck Browning
Blythe Danner	Tracy Ballard
Arthur Hill	Duffy
Yul Brynner	Gunslinger
Stuart Margolin	Harry
John Ryan	Dr. Schneider
Jim Antonio	Game show winner

Producers: Paul Lazarus III, James Aubrey; director: Richard Heffron; screenplay: Mayo Simon, George Schenck; photography: Howard Schwartz, Gene Polito, Robert Jessup; editor: James Mitchell; music: Fred Karlin; art direction: Trevor Williams; set direction: Dennis Peeples, Marvin March; sound: Charlie Knight; special effects: Brent Sellstrom; assistant director: Robert Koster; running time: 104 minutes.

THE ULTIMATE WARRIOR (1975)

Studio: Warner Brothers
Cast:

Yul Brynner, Max Von Sydow, Joanna Miles, William Smith, Richard Kelton, Stephen McHattie

Producers: Fred Weintraub, Paul Heller; director: Robert Clouse; screenplay: Robert Clouse; photography: Donald Hirshfield; music: Gil Melle; running time: 94 minutes.

— INDEX —

— Index —